1295

Meaning by Shakespeare

Developing the arguments of the same author's *That Shakespeherian Rag* (1985), these essays put the case that Shakespeare's plays have no essential meanings, but function as resources which we use to generate meaning for our own purposes. *A Midsummer Night's Dream, Measure for Measure, Coriolanus*, and *King Lear* are examined as concrete instances of the covert process whereby, in the twenthieth century, Shakespeare doesn't mean: *we* mean *by* Shakespeare.

Terence Hawkes is Professor of English at the University of Wales, Cardiff. A well known literary critic and theorist, he is General Editor of the *New Accents* series, and editor of the journal *Textual Practice*.

Meaning by Shakespeare

Terence Hawkes

London and New York

First published 1992
by Routledge
11 New Fetter Lane, London EC4P 4EE

Simultaneously published in the USA and Canada
by Routledge
a division of Routledge, Chapman and Hall, Inc.
29 West 35th Street, New York, NY 10001

Typeset in 10 on 12 point Palatino by
Ponting-Green Publishing Services, Sunninghill, Berks
Printed in Great Britain by
Clays Ltd, St Ives plc

British Library Cataloguing in Publication Data

A catalogue record for this book is available from the British Library.

Library of Congress Cataloging in Publication Data
Hawkes, Terence.
    Meaning by Shakespeare/Terence Hawkes.
        p.   cm.
    Includes bibliographical references and index.
    1. Shakespeare, William, 1564–1616—Criticism and interpretation.
    2. Reader–response criticism.   I. Title.
    PR2976.H384   1992
    823.3'3—dc20   92-7226

ISBN 0–415–07450–9   ISBN 0–415–07451–7 (pbk)

To Ann, once more

Contents

Acknowledgements

It suits the theme of this collection that some of the essays contained in it, written over the last six years, should have started life anchored to specific contexts. Conceived separately, they nevertheless share, I hope, a recognizable family likeness linking them with those composed with this volume in mind, as well as a point of view which makes it appropriate to bring them all together.

A version of 'Take me to your Leda' has appeared in *Shakespeare Survey 40*. A version of 'Lear's maps' has appeared in *Shakespeare Jahrbuch (West) 1989*. A version of 'Bardbiz' has appeared in *The London Review of Books*. Occasionally, I have drawn on and refashioned material previously contributed, in a different form, to *The Encyclopedia of Literature and Criticism* (Routledge, 1990) and *The Times Literary Supplement*. Relevant details are given below and I am grateful to the editors and publishers concerned for permission, where necessary, to reprint. Permission to quote material from T. S. Eliot's *Collected Poems*, his *Poems Written in Early Youth*, and from *The Letters of T. S. Eliot*, vol. 1 (ed. Valerie Eliot), has been granted by Mrs Valerie Eliot, the Eliot Estate, Harcourt Brace Jovanovich, Inc. and Faber & Faber Ltd. Unless otherwise specified, references to Shakespeare's plays are to the Arden edition in each case.

A number of individuals took the trouble to read or listen to versions of various portions of this material and I am extremely grateful to them for comments which were invariably helpful and frequently electrifying. They include John Drakakis, Malcolm Evans, Howard Felperin, Margreta de Grazia, Jean Howard, Marion Trousdale, Tamsin Spargo, Robert Stradling, Scott Newton, John Hartley and David Hawkes. This does not mean that they necessarily endorse any of my views. Needless to say, all errors are my own.

My colleagues and students in the Cardiff Centre for Critical and Cultural Theory already know how much I rely on their extensive knowledge and cheerful willingness to share it. I am especially grateful to both Catherine Belsey and Christopher Norris who have, as usual, made their scholarship, critical acumen, and unfailing good humour freely available to me. The staff of the Folger Shakespeare Library in Washington D.C. were models of helpful efficiency during an all too brief visit in the summer of 1990. Janice Price, tolerant, shrewd and most convivial of publishers, deserves a better book.

My greatest debt of gratitude remains, as always, to my wife.

T.H.
University of Wales
Cardiff

1   By

Ophelia: What means this my lord?
Hamlet: Marry, this is *miching malicho*. It means mischief.

(III, ii, 134–5)

Into the Mousetrap

The Prince's reply has more than a touch of mischief about it. Ophelia's question is about the dumb-show that precedes the performance of *The Murder of Gonzago*. She wants to know what such an 'inexplicable' (l. 12) pantomime signifies, the extent to which 'this show imports the argument of the play' (l. 136). As the spectacle ends and the actor playing the Prologue strides forth, she nervously raises the issue of signification again: 'Will 'a tell us what this show meant?' (l. 139). The oddity of Hamlet's response to Ophelia's question comes about because he chooses to answer it from a slightly different ground. In the process, he introduces a dimension of the word 'means' that she had not thought to reach.

Ophelia's focus is on what might be termed the argument of the play 'itself', on the essential, unchanging message she presumes that it carries, one which actors or critics like Hamlet can be looked to to expound. Hamlet's own view of that sense of meaning is derisive. The mild initial expletive of his reply is suddenly shocking in this context: 'Marry'. Is he really going to answer Ophelia's query about signification head-on? Is 'Marry' the daring opening of a carefully aimed tirade? Is it a verb, the one the play seems to turn on? Will Hamlet use it to point out that the dumb-show mimes the tragic history of one marriage and his mother's subsequent decision to marry a second time? No: that nerve is merely touched, not probed, and the rest of the sentence quickly shifts into an opposite mode. There will be no direct engagement with 'meaning' on the level

Ophelia intends. Far from it. A tricky phrase in a different language quickly mocks and deflects her query.

What does Hamlet's reply itself mean? On one level, *miching malicho* means something like 'sneaking mischief', and to some extent, particularly if 'this' refers to the dumb-show, it could be said to supply what has been asked for.[1] But the phrase's alien nature also muffles that purpose. As a result, with its signifying function barely operative, an unexpended energy propels it willy-nilly into a new and potentially even more disturbing realm of 'meaning': that of a non-discursive alliterative pattern – initiated by 'Marry'– whose accumulating urgency ultimately puts an extra sardonic spin on the word 'means'. As a result, the final statement 'It means mischief' triumphantly bursts the boundaries – the irony is incisive – of the sort of precision Ophelia is looking for.

What does 'It means mischief' mean? Does it offer an assessment of the content of the dumb-show? Or does it glance forward to sum up 'the argument of the play'? Do the words 'it means' introduce a translation of *miching malicho*, pulled back along that path by the alliteration? Or does the same alliteration push the phrase in an opposite direction, so that it blossoms as the final, unsettling flourish of a deliberately disconcerting figure? Overall, the effect is certainly to undermine any innocent gesture 'it means' may make towards straightforward explication – and for good reason. That sort of 'meaning' has after all proved cheap enough at Elsinore. The Prologue, Hamlet promises Ophelia, will turn out to be profligate in exactly those terms. He will not only tell us what the show means, he will, like Claudius, like Polonius, explain the 'meaning' of anything and everything:

> Ay, or any show that you will show him. Be not you asham'd to show, he'll not shame to tell you what it means.
>
> (III, ii, 140–1)

But Hamlet's answer also contains the possibility of a different notion of 'meaning'. If there was any 'essential' meaning embodied in *The Murder of Gonzago*, it has quite dissolved by the time the play confronts its audience at Elsinore. In that context, and triggered by Hamlet's addition of some lines to the text, it has turned into something very different. In consequence, the Prince's comment that 'It means mischief' can readily refer to what the play *intends now*, as a result of Hamlet's intervention; to what it is *up to*, here in Elsinore; to what, on this occasion, at this time and in this place, it *means to do*. The source of 'meaning' in this light appears almost to have migrated from the play 'itself' to the material context in which it is performed. Here and now, Hamlet seems to say to Ophelia, this is where 'meaning' will be generated: at the point where *The Murder of Gonzago* turns into *The Mousetrap*.

Marking the play

The essays which follow share a point of view developed in a previous collection, *That Shakespeherian Rag* (1986). Drawing on a series of engagements with the work of influential critics, the earlier book questioned whether we could have any genuine access to final, authoritative or essential meanings in respect of Shakespeare's plays. Implicitly and explicitly, it put the case that, like it or not, all we can ever do is use Shakespeare as a powerful element in specific ideological strategies.

The essays in *Meaning by Shakespeare* aim to probe some further implications of that position. The book's title attempts a slight sharpening of focus. Traditionally, critics, producers, actors and audiences of Shakespeare have assumed, with Ophelia, that the 'meaning' of each play is bequeathed to it *ab initio* and lies – artfully concealed perhaps – within its text. Each account, or production of the play, then offers to discover and lay hold of this meaning, hoisting it triumphantly, like buried treasure, into view. It is as if, to the information which used to be given in theatrical programmes, 'Cigarettes by Abdullah, Costumes by Motley, Music by Mendelssohn', we should add 'Meaning by Shakespeare'.

However, these essays rest on a different, almost opposite principle which, undertaken in the spirit of Hamlet's corrosive play on 'meaning', also involves a reconsideration of the word 'by'. The issues at stake can be simply put. Suppose we have no access to any 'essential' meaning nestling within Shakespeare's texts and awaiting our discovery (any more, let it be said, than Shakespeare did). Then what can their purpose be? If they do not transmit the meaning intended and embodied within them by their author, what on earth do Shakespeare's plays do? How do they work? And what are they *for*?

The answers proposed here suggest that, for us, the plays have the same function as, and work like, the words of which they are made. We *use* them in order to generate meaning. In the twentieth century, Shakespeare's plays have become one of the central agencies through which our culture performs this operation. That is what they do, that is how they work, and that is what they are for. Shakespeare doesn't mean: *we* mean *by* Shakespeare.

Hamlet offers a good example. At one time, this must obviously have been an interesting play written by a promising Elizabethan playwright. However, equally obviously, that is no longer the case. Over the years, *Hamlet* has taken on a huge and complex symbolizing function and, as a part of the institution called 'English literature', it has become far more than a mere play by a mere playwright. Issuing from one of the key components of that institution, not Shakespeare, but the creature 'Shakespeare', it has been transformed into the utterance of an oracle, the lucubration of a sage, the masterpiece of a poet-philosopher replete with transcendent wisdom about the way things are, always have been, and presumably always will be.

It is a condition which intensifies when 'English literature' is itself located within a system of mass education linking Britain, North America and the so-called Commonwealth countries. Then, together with a number of other texts, *Hamlet* acquires a central role in a complex programme of educational classification and social advancement. The more competence candidates show in discussing the Prince's lack of that quality, the greater their reward. No wonder that, at the end of their interchange about *The Mousetrap*, Ophelia begins to sound to us like an examiner. 'You are naught, you are naught', she admonishes Hamlet, 'I'll mark the play'.[2]

Hamlet scores high marks, inevitably. It comes to function as a universal cultural reference point, a piece of social shorthand. Bits of its language embed themselves in everyday speech until it starts to seem like a web of quotations. In the end, it enters our way of life as one of the resources through which that way of life generates meaning. As an aspect of the works of 'Shakespeare', the play helps to shape large categories of thought, particularly those which inform political and moral stances, modes and types of relationship, our ideas of how men and women, fathers and mothers, husbands and wives, uncles and nephews, sons and daughters ought respectively to behave and interact. It becomes part of a means of first formulating and then validating important power relationships, say between politicians and intellectuals, soldiers and students, the world of action and that of contemplation. Perhaps its probing of the relation between art and social life, role-playing on stage and role-playing in society, appears so powerfully to offer an adequate account of important aspects of our own experience that it ends by constructing them. In other words, *Hamlet* crucially helps to determine how we perceive and respond to the world in which we live. You can even name a cigar after it.

A pragmatism

This is to see art as one of the major activities through which a society 'means': that is, makes the world a significant and habitable space by defining for itself and distinguishing between crucial categories whose status is otherwise indeterminate. What, for instance, do we mean by 'man', by 'woman', by 'duty', by 'justice', by 'nation', by 'honour', by 'marriage', by 'love'? These are far from simple issues, yet our whole way of life depends on our answers to such questions: they give our culture its distinctive identity at a particular historical juncture. To study *Hamlet* is to be invited to consider and to reinforce or perhaps to contest and undermine inherited meanings of that order of importance.

Of course, the institution of literature is not the only agency through which those meanings are generated, reinforced or contested. Other activities – they involve music, song, social dancing, sport, domestic architecture, modes of cooking, political pamphlets, parliamentary debates, legal wrangles, the whole range of what people actually get up to in the material world in which they live – might also claim to offer 'texts' matching in fruitfulness those of novels, plays and poems. They might even propose the validity of a quite differently contoured world, through their record of a pattern of strategically mounted resistance to the established one. Certainly, they indicate that a society's dominant presentation of itself will often mask what it derives from: tensions between opposing factions, systematic projects of exclusion, the discouraging, even the suppression, of dissent. The most obvious result of such a challenge from the so-called 'periphery' has been the questioning in recent years of literature's claims to centrality and to transcendence. In the case of Shakespeare, the suggestion that a play may speak 'for an age' begins to seem overweening. That it could speak 'for all time' appears suddenly absurd.

In addition, powerful arguments have invited a reassessment of what might be termed literature's raw material, the individual text produced by a particular author. One of the major effects of latter-day post-structuralist thinking has been the subversion of a central ideological commitment to the idea of the individual, sovereign self, the human 'subject', as the fundamental unit of existence and the main negotiable instrument of meaning. In consequence, the notion of the text as the direct expression of that subject's innermost thoughts and feelings has also been undermined. And amongst the first casualties of that development is the supposed 'authenticity' of the text as a document whose final 'meaning' includes unmediated access to its author's intimate being.

With the text's 'authority' and 'authenticity' so fundamentally questioned in this way, it has become more and more difficult to claim that *Hamlet* offers once-for-all revelations about what Shakespeare 'thought' and 'felt' with regard to the events and characters the play seems to deploy, or to assume that the 'meaning' of the play should be limited to or by whatever Shakespeare intended to say 'through' it. This is not to say that the text known as *Hamlet* no longer materially exists. But it is to say that our way of describing, of accounting for, of establishing a productive purchase on that text must change. And the change will effectively serve to push the play's material existence into the foreground. For if *Hamlet*, like *The Murder of Gonzago*, offers no determinable set of essential meanings, it demands nevertheless to be seen as the *occasion* of a number of meanings which have been attributed to it at various moments in the past as well as the present. The Prince's mobilization of *The Murder of Gonzago* as *The Mousetrap* could hardly be bettered as an instance of that process and a measure of its potential impact. There are no essential, transcendental meanings here. *The Mousetrap*'s mode is determinedly occasional. An intention to 'mean mischief' is precisely the earnest of a commitment to material political intervention in a way of life, to the premeditated appropriation of specific cultural instruments, for specific purposes, in a particular social context. On this basis, *miching malicho* means taking part.

The idea that a play can and inevitably does take part in the affairs of a society requires an abandonment of the notion of the primacy or, in practical terms, of the existence of any transcendental 'meaning' located within it, able finally to subsume, surpass or determine all others. It calls instead for a recognition of the degree to which all texts are contextualized by history. And that leads in the direction of what might be called a literary pragmatism: the notion that all texts have something in common with *The Mousetrap*. That is, they always 'take part' in historical milieux, whenever and however they are realized, either initially or subsequently. As a result, no final context-free meaning or 'truth' can, should, or need be assigned to them.

This 'historicist', or 'anti-essentialist', or 'holistic' position evidently owes a good deal to the ideas of some American philosophers, from William James and John Dewey to Richard Rorty, as well as to those of some German-speaking philosophers from Nietzsche and Heidegger to the later Wittgenstein. The notion of 'meaning by' has obvious roots in that work, most of it a direct challenge to the presuppositions of the broad sweep of current literary criticism written in English.[3] There are no surprises here. Amongst the essays which follow, 'Take me to your Leda' will make the point that, with a phenomenon as internal to a culture as Shakespeare is to that of Britain, the outsider's view – European or American – has often proved a helpful one. Pragmatism's transatlantic provenance even hints at the continuation of a wider and mutually instructive Anglo-American relationship of long standing. T. S. Eliot's curious role in it forms the subject of another essay.

Such a position does not of course imply that a text's meaning is finally determined by the historical context in which it initially appears. That limited notion of historicism must always yield to the view that human beings are permanently involved in a continuing process of meaning-making, one to which all texts, as aspects of human culture, are always subject, and beyond which they may be conceivable but will remain ungraspable. To attempt to grasp them at all, as the essay on *A Midsummer Night's Dream* tries to show, is inevitably to become involved in the making of meaning in a particular context.

The idea that meaning is made rather than found has roots in European thought which reach back at least to the time of Vico, and it should be allowed to add its full social and moral weight to the sense of what 'taking part' implies. Its essentialist opposite, what Dewey called the 'spectator theory of knowledge', will always be undercut both by the instability of the pseudo-polarity which offers to separate spectator from participant and, in my own view, by the undesirability of the politics which seek to sustain it. We should know by now that a 'spectator theory of society' is a recipe for, as well as a consequence of, totalitarianism. A contrary theory whereby spectators merge into participants – a theme discernible in *A Midsummer Night's Dream* and many other plays of the period to a degree which invites a 'pragmatic' account of them – invokes a political commitment concerning the involvement of members of a culture in the shaping of its way of life, to which literary criticism ought not to be blind. For Richard Rorty at least, to take part in the broad reactive social process registered and reinforced by such a motif is to engage with the large-scale and continuing cultural dialogue or 'conversation' which constitutes the very precondition of democracy.[4]

What passes amongst some literary critics for a text's 'real' meaning can only be a temporary pause in this otherwise healthy process. And it seems harsh, in its name, to deny to subsequent audiences and readers what Shakespeare's plays apparently freely grant to those – from the Prince of Denmark to Bottom the Weaver – who set themselves to 'mean by' texts within them. A text is surely better served if it is perceived not as the embodiment of some frozen, definitive significance, but as a kind of intersection or confluence which is continually traversed, a no-man's land, an arena, in which different and opposed readings, urged from different and opposed political positions, compete in history for ideological power: the power, that is, to determine cultural meaning – to say what the world is and should be like. We try to make *Hamlet* mean for our purposes now: others will try to make it mean differently for their purposes then (or now). The 'conversation'– albeit of a harsher, more overtly political nature than Rorty perhaps allows – continues.[5] But there is no final, essential or 'real' meaning at the end of it. There is no end. There is only and always the business of 'meaning by'.

Enter the Prince

In terms of literary criticism, a general movement which favours the principle of historical contextualization has recently become discernible on both sides of the Atlantic and the essay 'Lear's maps' tries to situate the present arguments in relation to it. Labelled as New Historicism in America and as Cultural Materialism in Britain, both forms of historicism are conceived in opposition to the sort of criticism which privileges an idealized, context-free 'literature' and, as part of it, constructs a heroically transcendent 'Shakespeare', whose works deal in truths that are true for all time.

If this kind of idealism appears in its strongest form in Coleridge's reading of Shakespeare made nearly two hundred years ago, most teachers of English can confirm that it persists, surprisingly enough, as the common coin of popular, and indeed certain academic responses to the Bard, well into the twentieth century. The oddly protracted correspondence which followed the appearance of the essay 'Bardbiz' in *The London Review of Books* gives ample evidence of that. I have included a slightly modified version of that piece here for a number of reasons. In pressing home some of the issues developed more loosely in the essays which precede it, perhaps it can stand as a focusing *reprise* of the general argument. In treating the work of other, rather differently orientated critics, it might help to locate that argument in a broader and more interesting context. And in generating a wide-ranging discussion that ultimately probed surprisingly large matters of cultural politics both in Britain and abroad, it may finally suggest something of the degree to which the Bard continues to offer a central forum wherein, from competing positions, far-reaching and complex transactions of 'meaning by' are still negoti-ated. Bardbiz remains everybody's business.

As the twentieth century approaches its close, those with a taste for the processes by which cultural meanings have been most powerfully generated in it may well find themselves drawn to Stratford-upon-Avon. Amongst the delights of that venue, the celebrations surrounding Shakespeare's Birthday, held each year on 23 April, quickly acquire memorable stature. The essay 'Shakespeare and the General Strike' offers a modest glimpse of the riches they afforded over sixty years ago. It is a pleasure to report that the rate at which these continue to multiply shows no sign of slackening.

On 23 April 1991, the annual Shakespeare's Birthday Lecture was delivered in Stratford by the Prince of Wales. Speaking from the stage of the Swan Theatre, he mounted what the newspapers called an 'outspoken attack' on the nation's educational standards and the growing neglect of what he termed 'the cultural heritage of our country' (*The Independent*, 23 April 1991, p. 1).

'It is almost incredible', the Prince lamented, 'that, in Shake-speare's land, one child in seven leaves primary school functionally illiterate.' We are, he added, in danger of producing 'an entire generation of culturally disinherited young people'. In the face of so-called education experts, we should, he went on, 'screw our courage to the sticking place' and defiantly insist that they are talking nonsense. For there are, he concluded,

> several GCSE English literature courses which prescribe no Shake-speare at all. There is at least one A-level English literature syllabus on which Shakespeare is not compulsory. . . . Thousands of intelligent children leaving school at sixteen have never seen a play of Shakespeare on film or on the stage, and have never been asked to read a single word of any one of his plays.
>
> (*The Independent*, 23 April 1991, p. 2)

The central point, that Shakespeare's plays have an essential, culture-reinforcing, morally-uplifting and context-free set of 'mean-ings' permanently on offer, is resoundingly made in tones that Coleridge (the later Coleridge anyway) would have recognized and admired. Few of the educationists who rushed to deny or confirm such deprivation bothered to consider that the very conditions the Prince despaired of – illiteracy, never having seen a Shakespeare play, never having read a word of the Bard – were perhaps part of the material context in which most Elizabethans lived, and that in themselves they helped to constitute fundamental aspects of the culture that made Shakespeare possible. Even fewer seemed ready or willing to contextualize the Prince's remarks themselves.

That these issued from the heir to the British throne, speaking from the centre of Britain, at the birthplace of the national poet, and on the latter's birthday may not be finally significant. That the address was made in the name of and to the members of a culture whose 'heritage', it can be daily seen, is currently far more complex and far less Euro-centric than has been presupposed, may be barely relevant. That it was made in the face of, almost on the eve of, the integration of 'Shakespeare's land' into a larger Community whose embrace threatens a much-trumpeted loss of national identity, may be almost beside the point. But put together, these factors might at the very least suggest that we ponder not what Shakespeare means, but what the Prince of Wales meant by him here, at this time, in this place, on this occasion. *Miching malicho*, perhaps? Of course that, as the following essays suggest, is not the sole preserve of Princes. In fact, in the present context, I will take it as my cue.

2 Or

Nedar

I can begin by unveiling some Shakespearean words never before seen or heard:

> And last, forget not that I nurtured you
> Till, pouring forth your beauty, uncasked then
> For other palates' savour, you were drawn
> Down into new blood and, embodied thence,
> Sprang wondrous free beyond your parent's power.

The lines are to be spoken by one of the characters in *A Midsummer Night's Dream*. Let me introduce Nedar.

Nedar is one of Helena's parents. The name is not English, certainly not quintessentially so in the way that the non-Greek names in the play such as Bottom, Snug, or Peter Quince obviously aim to be. But the name Nedar does not occur in the Ancient Greek world either, and so can scarcely claim derivation from the play's world of Athens. Ovid calls Helen (of Troy) 'Tyndar's daughter', a reference to King Tyndareos of Sparta, and T. Walter Herbert hears an echo of that in Nedar's name – though the matter is complicated by the story which nominates Zeus (disguised as a swan) as her genuine father.[1]

If Greekness at that more exalted level suggests fertile ground, then we might note that Zeus's Helen certainly haunts this play's Helena in the form of glancing references. Demetrius, waking with the love-juice in his eyes, perceives the formerly scorned Helena anew as 'O Helen, goddess, nymph, perfect, divine!' (III, ii, 137) – a description which annoys the recipient, since she takes it for a joke. Later, Theseus's denunciation of imaginative excess complains of the lover who 'Sees Helen's beauty in a brow of Egypt' (V, i, 11), and in the performance of *Pyramus and Thisbe*, Thisbe offers to be 'trusty' 'like Helen, till the Fates me kill' (V, i, 195) – presumably intending to refer to Hero. But these references, whatever else they signal, offer no link with Nedar. Perhaps they serve merely to reinforce the point that the play's gawky, 'painted maypole' (III, ii, 296) is hardly Helen of Troy.

Until now, Nedar has had no lines to utter in the play. But if that silence, like all silences, speaks, its topic must be ownership. For Nedar's name is only ever presented in the possessive mode: its two formulations in the play are first, Lysander's assertion that

> Demetrius, I'll avouch it to his head,
> Made love to Nedar's daughter, Helena
> (I, i, 106–7)

and second, Egeus's recognition that

> My lord, this is my daughter here asleep,
> And this Lysander; this Demetrius is,
> This Helena, old Nedar's Helena.
> (IV, i, 127–9)

In the play's terms, this mode seems wholly appropriate and it apparently accords with the filial ambience of an Athens in which daughters are more or less wholly owned, as property, by their fathers, to be disposed of according to their will. Egeus, Hermia's father, makes this perfectly clear. Hermia's 'obedience' is legally 'due' to him, and he begs 'the ancient privilege of Athens' that 'As she is mine, I may dispose of her' (I, i, 37–41). Indeed, the relation is exactly one of property:

> she is mine, and all my right of her
> I do estate unto Demetrius.
> (I, i, 97–8)

Theseus, recently successful in a war against the matriarchal society of the Amazons (Plutarch records that he eventually married an Amazon named Hyppolita, which concluded the war), confirms this absolute right in no uncertain terms, and in the process tells us a good deal about how daughters are regarded in his newly victorious patriarchy:

> What say you, Hermia? Be advis'd, fair maid.
> To you your father should be as a god:
> One that compos'd your beauties, yea, and one

To whom you are but as a form in wax
By him imprinted, and within his power
To leave the figure, or disfigure it.

(I, i, 46–51)

That appalling metaphor – no less so if 'disfigure' means to change rather than wound – gives the full weight of the paternal power at stake in this kind of property relationship. Mothers clearly have no part in it.[2] And when Peter Quince later uses the word in what is presumably a malapropism,

> one must come in with a bush of thorns and a lantern, and say he comes to disfigure or to present the person of Moonshine.

(III, i, 55ff.)

– it casually disgorges its subtext, speaking of the forcible manipulation of physical appearance and so generating the same slight *frisson* of horror despite – or maybe because of – its overtly comic context. The only right any daughter retained in this society was – again a sort of 'property' right – her 'virgin patent' (I, i, 80).

Older women

If they have considered Nedar at all, most readers of the play will have done so on the basis of a major assumption, that the name refers to Helena's father. However, the lines I have composed, Hamlet-like, above, obviously challenge that. They do so because the grounds for assuming Nedar's maleness – if any – are dubious. The nearest version of the name in Ancient Greece exists as 'Neda', the name of a river, and, presumably before that, of a nymph associated – interestingly enough – with Zeus. In that form, 'Neda' is of course female. An 'old Neda' could easily be Helena's mother.

Surprisingly perhaps, for a play so taken up with youth, love, procreation and marriage, *A Midsummer Night's Dream* seems haunted by the shadowy images of older women. The play begins with Theseus complaining, like an impetuous legatee, of

> how slow
> This old moon wanes! She lingers my desires,
> Like to a step-dame or a dowager
> Long withering out a young man's revenue.

(I, i, 3–6)

Of course, 'dowagers', older women who possess 'endowments' or sums of 'revenue', can be benign creatures. Lysander's elopement with Hermia will be facilitated by such a 'widow aunt',

> a dowager
> Of great revenue, and she hath no child –
> From Athens is her house remote seven leagues –
> And she respects me as her only son.
>
> (I, i, 157–60)

But these women are largely invisible, excluded from the main action and firmly exiled to its borders. I am not here drawing on those 'silences' in the play whose very existence is mocked by Richard Levin, in which the text is said actively to 'repress' or 'conceal' a feminine or maternal 'subtext', conflicting with and contradicting the imperatives of its patriarchal world.[3] The 'hidden mother' that Coppélia Kahn aims to retrieve in *King Lear* is perhaps suppressed in that play in a way that Nedar is not in this.[4] A personage called Nedar is not 'hidden', but overtly referred to twice in the text of *A Midsummer Night's Dream*.

Lysander's 'widow aunt', crucially important to the plot, has a similar claim to existence, even though she never appears on the stage. And she inhabits the same shadowy zone as Thisbe's mother (a part assigned to Robin Starveling, the tailor, in *Pyramus and Thisbe* (I, ii, 55)) who also never appears. The 'votaress' of Titania's order, the mother of the disputed changeling, whose 'swimming gait' in pregnancy is so strikingly reported (II, i, 130–4) dwells there too.

Of course, there are male absentees announced by the text: Pyramus's father (to be played by Tom Snout), Thisbe's father (a part claimed by Peter Quince), the Indian Boy demanded by both Oberon and Titania. But these are outweighed by a growing and finally tumultuous crowd of older women who gradually accumulate on the play's margins: the 'breathless housewives', the gossips, the 'wisest aunt, telling the saddest tale'(II, i, 37ff.) all routinely tricked by Puck, the 'ladies or Fair Ladies' (III, i, 38) congenitally afraid of swords and lions, confronted by Bottom and Snug, and the 'mothers' with whom the ambitious 'mother's sons' of the mechanicals consistently assert their filiation (I, ii, 73 and III, i, 69). All this takes place in the shadow of what Louis Adrian Montrose calls the 'pervasive cultural presence' of the ageing Queen Elizabeth, who functions as 'a condition of the play's imaginative possibility' and might even have been physically present as part of its first audience.[5]

If Nedar can thus reasonably claim a place amongst the play's host of banished older women, that perhaps draws attention to her curious name's final, seductive dimension. As an uncomplicated anagram of 'Arden', a Hellenized version of something essentially English, it effortlessly mingles aspects of the play's two worlds. And in the presence of a text committed to giving to airy nothing 'a local habitation and a name', we might remember that Arden was, of course, the family name of Shakespeare's mother.

One more time

The definition of what a mother is or may be forms a crucial concern for all cultures, none more so than the Elizabethan.[6] Montrose suggests that the period saw a concerted Protestant effort to appropriate the Virgin Mary's maternal symbolism and make it part of the mystique of the Virgin Queen. At the time of *A Midsummer Night's Dream*, Elizabeth was clearly an old woman. But in terms of the symbols with which ideologies work, her situation was massively paradoxical. Obviously mortal, she wore the monarchical mantle of immortality. Ageing, and so evidently subject to change, she embodied, as an emblem of monarchy, that notion of continuing sameness and political permanence asserted by her father's motto: *Eadem Semper.* For reasons of state a virgin, she was also that state's 'mother'.[7] In fact, within a very few years she would be replaced by a monarch the basis of whose authority was his opposite claim to be *parens patriae*, the father of his country.[8]

A Midsummer Night's Dream might be expected at least to engage with such paradoxes. Yet in respect of the obviously important issue of maternity, the play seems specifically to marginalize, if not exclude, the nurturing, vessel-like relationship of mother to child, which traditionally tempers the inseminating, constitutive and 'imprinting' role of the father. If Nedar is Helena's mother, her silence is eloquent in its reinforcement of Montrose's point that 'Hermia and Helena have no mothers; they have only fathers'.[9] In other words, in the immediate context in which the plot unfolds, the fundamental mother–daughter relationship which we might presume to have been the basis of the defeated Amazonian matriarchy over which Theseus triumphed before the play began, has been wholly suppressed by the time of his support of Egeus's claims. Whatever else the play has on offer, it is certainly not the delights or consolations of motherhood.

Indeed what is odd about Nedar – and what constitutes the basis for most readings' suppression even of the name – is that the character seems superfluous. As a parent, Nedar appears merely repetitive of a principle fully and powerfully presented elsewhere, perhaps in Egeus. The barely mentioned Nedar, in short, seems almost an excrescence, the merest adjunct, virtually redundant, surplus to requirements, a left-over perhaps from another version of the play, a nervous repetitive textual tic that could easily be removed and no one would notice. If Nedar had been given words to say, no doubt some editor would long ago have recommended their excision.

On that basis, excision waits in the wings for quite a lot of *A Midsummer Night's Dream*. For in its general style, the same sort of apparently gratuitous repetition that Nedar seems to represent, that promiscuous proliferation of additional ways of putting things, turns out to be a feature of the text which apparently cries out for pruning. Modern critics and editors, avid for unity of intention, purpose and meaning in these matters, persistently reach for their secateurs.

And yet the truth is that a repetitive mode invests the whole play, almost to an extent that seems to insist on repetition as one of its central concerns. Even at the end, it seems barely able to reach a conclusion, but splutters out with a succession of more or less conventional endings, one after the other. The main plot of *A Midsummer Night's Dream* ends after all with Act IV. Act V seems to some degree 'added' on in order to allow for the performance of another play. But even the emphatically signalled end of *Pyramus and Thisbe* ('Adieu, adieu, adieu' (V, i, 334)) is followed by Bottom's surprising 'starting up' to address the audience (V, i, 337). Then comes a Bergomask dance (V, i, 348), preferred to an 'epilogue' from the mechanicals; then the exit of Theseus, Hippolyta, the lovers and the Court (V, i, 356); then Puck's ritual sweeping of the stage with a broom (V, i, 357–76); then the sudden entry of Oberon, Titania and 'all their Train' (V, i, 377); then the song 'Now, until the break of day / Through this house each fairy stray. . .' (V, i, 387); and then Puck's final address to the audience, which is of course not final at all, since it would be followed by the reappearance of the whole cast to receive the audience's applause (V, i, 409–22).

The same 'spluttering' that marks the ending permeates the action of the play from the start. It offers to move forward purposefully enough:

> Now, fair Hippolyta, our nuptial hour
> Draws on apace; four happy days bring in
> Another moon
>
> (I, i, 1–3)

but Theseus goes quickly on to his complaint about the new moon being 'lingered' by an old moon. The course of the true love it describes may never run smooth, but neither does its exposition. Theseus began by wooing Hippolyta with his sword: now he will wed her in 'another key'. But, immediately after the order has been given to 'stir up the Athenian youth to merriments' (I, i, 12) in celebration of love's fruitfulness, Egeus enters, proposing to put his daughter to death unless a quite different set of nuptials takes place in accordance with his wish. And the lovers' later 'visions' and 'revisions' of each other are no less characteristic instances of the same stopping, starting, alternating and hiccuping mode.

Confusion generated by this process seems to soak through to the individual words of the text and to take its toll of the way these are read. A good example occurs with the multiple illustrations of his argument layered into Theseus's famous rationalist analysis of the lovers' story at the beginning of Act V:

> Lovers and madmen have such seething brains,
> Such shaping fantasies, that apprehend
> More than cool reason ever comprehends.
> The lunatic, the lover, and the poet
> Are of imagination all compact:
> One sees more devils than vast hell can hold;
> That is the madman: the lover, all as frantic,
> Sees Helen's beauty in a brow of Egypt:
> The poet's eye, in a fine frenzy rolling,
> Doth glance from heaven to earth, from earth to heaven;
> And as imagination bodies forth
> The form of things unknown, the poet's pen
> Turns them to shapes, and gives to airy nothing
> A local habitation and a name.
> Such tricks hath strong imagination,
> That if it would but apprehend some joy,
> It comprehends some bringer of that joy:
> Or, in the night, imagining some fear,
> How easy is a bush suppos'd a bear!
>
> (V, i, 4–22)

The last two lines have often proved too much for some twentieth-century critics who have proposed cutting what they see as a final, exasperating repetition.[10] Dover Wilson quotes R. G. White's comment 'Would Shakespeare, after thus reaching the climax of his thought, fall a-twaddling about bushes and bears?' and he notes the 'loss of dignity' in the rhythm caused by these lines, which he concludes must therefore have been interpolated.[11] E. K. Chambers, editing the play for the Warwick Shakespeare, concludes that 'These lines are rather bald after what they follow' and suggests that they are perhaps a survival from an earlier version of the play.[12] But David Young notes that the shift from blank verse to couplet which they embody is 'very characteristic of the play'.[13]

A plausible-sounding process of revision has been put forward in explanation of these repetitive features, and Dover Wilson has suggested that the two lines in question here are 'so poor' partly for this reason. Indeed, he cites the whole passage as a 'very beautiful' example of how the irregular verse-lining of this passage in the original Quarto can give us clues to the history of dramatic texts.[14]

But something is surely very wrong here. Far from being a mere superfluous addition to the speech, the lines

> Or, in the night, imagining some fear,
> How easy is a bush suppos'd a bear!

could be said genuinely to further its argument. Theseus is making the case that in those of 'strong imagination', the activity of 'apprehension', involving the imaginative generation of an emotion, leads almost immediately to its 'comprehension', by means of concrete actualization in the material world. This, he then claims, applies equally well to the two opposed spheres of joy on the one hand and fear on the other.

The word which is causing the trouble is one whose implications take us to the centre of the play: 'or'. As Theseus uses it here, 'or' links two polarities whilst maintaining the difference between them. The scholars who wish to excise it, however, are reading it lulled by the play's overriding repetitive rhythms, as if it invoked mere sameness. In short, they are reading 'or' as if it were 'and'.

In fact, 'and' could be said to be the opposite of 'or'. 'And' certainly proposes repetition, more of the same. But 'or' has a more disturbing function. It introduces alternatives, realignments, different possibilities, unconsidered consequences, surprising subsequence; it signals a worrying, revisionary and subversive current which sets itself against the progressive course announced by Theseus, committed to pushing forward, apace. If 'and' in general terms indicates 'the same', 'or' implies difference. Why should the larger rhythms of the play almost drown it out?

The first moments of *A Midsummer Night's Dream* are indeed peppered with 'or's and the complications and hesitancies they announce. Hermia is to be disposed of 'either to this gentleman/Or to her death' (I, i, 43–4). Her father has the power to 'leave ' her figure 'or disfigure it' (l. 51). She must decide 'either to die the death, or to abjure/For ever the society of men' (ll. 65–6), fit her fancies to her father's will 'Or else the law of Athens yields you up. . .To death, or to a vow of single life' (ll. 119–21). Even the recursive figures of stichomythia ring with 'or's undermining of the straight path of true love:

Lysander: The course of true love never did run smooth;
            But either it was different in blood –
Hermia: O cross! too high to be enthrall'd to low.
Lysander: Or else misgraffed in respect of years –
Hermia: O spite! too old to be engag'd to young.
Lysander: Or else it stood upon the choice of friends –
Hermia: O hell! to choose love by another's eyes.
Lysander: Or, if there were a sympathy in choice
            War, death, or sickness did lay siege to it
                                        (I, i, 134ff.)

Overtly, *A Midsummer Night's Dream* seems set on the celebration of unending repetition. It focuses not only on marriage and the continuing generation of children through which the society constantly renews itself, but also on the endless and endlessly fruitful cycle of the seasons which ensures that the festival of Midsummer Night comes around year after year. To compare medieval, or early modern culture with our own, an old historical perspective suggests, is to compare a circle with a straight line. A culture whose central mode is repetitive, whose circular and cyclical commitment to kingship, Christianity, orality and seasonal rotation involves it in the ceaseless generation of 'the same', contrasts sharply with that post-industrial way of life whose straightforward linear mode, inseparable from democracy, enlightenment, literacy and factory production, we inherit. Committed as it is to sameness, where ours is committed to change, such a culture might be said to be proposing an endless 'and'. *Eadem Semper* indeed.

But it might also be said that in tandem with the 'and' motif of permanent recurrence, *A Midsummer Night's Dream* also covertly offers to engage with an opposite mode represented by the word 'or'. It is one in which repetition – presupposing though it does sameness, absence either of change or difference – ironically also generates the conditions in which change must occur. To return to the older women which the play seems bent on excluding, this suggests that we might probe beyond the notion that they simply indicate the degree and extent to which women are excluded and degraded in a patriarchal society. Perhaps a deeper level of exclusion also operates, one which gives some reason for the first.

In a society committed to the preservation of things as they are, ageing, particularly the ageing of women, and specifically the ageing of a woman monarch, points to an ineluctable, opposite and feared principle of irrevocable change. The process of growing older, of becoming inevitably barren, will always challenge and even contradict the endlessly repetitive, permanently fruitful modes indicated by the eternal return of Midsummer and the constant reproduction, through children, of human society. A play which banishes older women to its margins is banishing those in whom the linear processes of life have brought about what we still crudely stigmatize as an unpalatable 'change'. In the modern word 'menopause' there lingers the notion that far from being an acceptable and organic inheritance of women, the 'change' introduces an inappropriate hiatus and final cessation of the 'natural' monthly cycle for which women were properly and permanently designed.[15] By this, a 'menopausal' woman can still only be defined negatively. Far from embodying a positive stage of development, she apparently turns into a creature in whom a fundamental process has permanently paused. The Elizabethan vocabulary contains no word that adequately describes this changed condition. In its own way, perhaps *A Midsummer Night's Dream* is offering its reiterated 'and' as a bulwark against an unavoidable 'or' of literally unspeakable enormity. And if the play hints that this is partly what we may 'mean by' it, it turns into a cruel enough celebration for a wedding.

Same difference

That might serve to remind us once more that the new world order constructed by Theseus has a disturbing commitment to a complex notion of 'disfiguring'. It extends from the threatened violence with which Hermia is confronted, to the gentler spectacle of actors who 'disfigure' themselves by dressing up as Walls, Moons and Lions, a process which in one case leads to a grotesque 'translation' from one species to another. In fact, a motif of disfiguring, translating change is all-pervasive. It could even be said that *A Midsummer Night's Dream* invests wholesale in metamorphosis to the extent that the change it most powerfully chronicles is one to which the art of drama particularly lends itself: the repeated metamorphosis of spectators into participants. This happens on and off the stage. Oberon both observes and participates in the interrelationships of the lovers. He acts as 'audience' to as well as participant in Titania's duping. Theseus, Hippolyta and their court constitute a famously participating audience for the performance of *Pyramus and Thisbe*, and Puck has, of course, been first a spectator of and then a participant in the rehearsals for that play: 'I'll be an auditor;/An actor too perhaps, if I see cause' (III, i, 75–6). Finally, when, at the end of *A Midsummer Night's Dream* itself, Puck addresses its larger audience in the theatre,

> So, goodnight unto you all.
> Give me your hands, if we be friends,
> And Robin shall restore amends.
>
> (V, i, 422–4)

the applause which now enters the play's actual content, completes and confirms those spectators' transformation into participants and aptly concludes the play.

It is therefore entirely appropriate that, at the height of the action, Helena should recall and foreground an idyllic, change-free 'sameness' which once seemed able to contain and resolve all the differences in the world:

> We, Hermia, like two artificial gods,
> Have with our needles created both one flower,
> Both on one sampler, sitting on one cushion,
> Both warbling of one song, both in one key,
> As if our hands, our sides, voices and minds,
> Had been incorporate. So we grew together,
> Like to a double cherry, seeming parted,
> But yet an union in partition,
> Two lovely berries moulded on one stem;
> So, with two seeming bodies, but one heart;
>
> (III, ii, 203–12)

But that state is now over and 'all forgot' (ll. 201–2). Change and distinction reign, differences and particularities abound, men can and do choose between Helena and Hermia and their relationship is utterly altered as a result. In this sense, the process of 'disfiguring' or radical, revisionary change constitutes a major dimension of the play and for that reason most commentators have rightly seen Ovid's *Metamorphoses* as a considerable influence upon it.

But the mechanism of change in the *Metamorphoses* is a far from simple matter. For not only do Ovid's stories chronicle physical changes on a massive scale, they also in their telling embody a structural principle of change through an extensive use of the rhetorical mode of *digressio*. As a result, these are not straightforward narratives. Repetition, recapitulation, hesitation, circularity, starting and restarting, the embedding of stories within stories, a wholesale refusal of simple linear progression, these are as much the characteristics of the *Metamorphoses*, as they are of an older, pre-Socratic and pre-literate world at large, to which Ovid had access.[16] Moreover, the stories are not new, but collected and recycled from a wide range of sources. Marshall McLuhan has made the case that the process of multifarious 'disfigurement' which the stories recount, finds itself echoed in the kind of narration which realizes them, and the circulating, repetitive mode in which it takes place.

As a result, a major paradox emerges: repetition, or the generation of more of the same, itself becomes the basis for change and the construction of difference. 'Ovid is the re-teller of tales. It is the re-telling that is the metamorphosis.' In McLuhan's view, this derives from a broader principle, whereby the cessation of some activity, followed by its repetition, actually serves to bring change about: 'the technique of metamorphosis is quite simply that of the *arrest*, the interval, whether of space or time or rhythm. It is this that causes the change or metamorphosis. So, even a replay in football acts as a metamorphosis.'[17]

McLuhan saw Ovid as an unrecognized but deeply significant influence on the writings of post-Symbolist artists such as Joyce, Eliot and Pound, one which partly manifested itself in the characteristic Symbolist interest in the disruption of linear sequence and the suppression of 'connectives'.[18] The halting of sequence, and the 'double-take' or repetition which that brings about, has the effect of making us aware of our usual dependence on linearity and sequential progression. This awareness produces (even constitutes) change because it generates a new and disconcerting awareness of our present environment and of its otherwise unnoticed effects upon us. From the Romantics on, repetition, recuperation, appears as the crucial mode of an art whose aim is to sensitize its audience to its environment, and thus effect a revolutionary change in awareness and response. For Wordsworth, the basis of a poetry appropriate to such a purpose was to be its expression of emotion *recollected* in tranquillity. Far from acting as a bulwark against 'or', the repetitive, recycling, revisionary activity represented by 'and' helps to produce it.

In *A Midsummer Night's Dream*, a similar Ovidean principle seems to operate at the play's heart. Its halting, disruptive and repetitive mode has been noticed. And as the plot unfolds, change seems to spring from the very stratagems designed to maintain sameness, to the dismay of those caught up in the process. The very idea of filial generation, for example, whereby a father 'imprints' a 'form in wax', deals in an evident sense of repetition through the metaphor of 'reproduction', and its links with 'printing' and 'reprinting'.[19] Yet, as Egeus discovers, the notion that parents can thus safely 'repeat' themselves in their children runs full tilt into its opposite when the children seek to undertake liaisons in the world beyond the family. In fact, a central paradox emerges whereby the process of filiation, committed to an 'imprinting' repetition of the same, inevitably leads on to a social process of affiliation, through marriage in this case, which must, willy-nilly, be committed to difference.[20]

The naming of parts

A calculated feature of the complex of paradoxes inhabiting the *Metamorphoses* is that its chronicle of fundamental change from same to different (initially even from Chaos to Order, from Golden Age to Silver, Bronze and Iron) as well as its multifarious exercises in digression, proceeds by means of what it serenely claims to be an 'unbroken thread' of verse. Its commitment to continuity, to going on unchangingly linking story of change to story of change, continually 'replaying' its theme of radical alteration, constitutes a final and unifying structural feature. Here the distinction between 'and' and 'or' is playfully elided to justify the final paradoxical claim made by the author that, as a result of the complex manoeuvres of chronicling change, he will remain always the same. The repetitions of 'and' may normally and inevitably result in 'or' but in his case, the reverse will happen. 'Or' will lead to 'and'. The stories he tells of change will ensure that he remains the same forever, achieving a kind of personal immortality: '...my name will be imperishable .... If there be any truth in poets' prophecies, I shall live to all eternity, immortalized by fame'.[21]

In an Elizabethan context, Ovid's pretensions seem at first sight to have some validity, and the poet's claim that 'my name will be imperishable' invites confirmation. Names seem obvious bulwarks against fundamental metamorphosis because they appear to deal, in this play at least, in the unchanging essences of their bearers. That is, they frequently invoke an ancient principle whereby 'name' reflects 'nature' which Harry Levin has aptly dubbed 'psychological ono-matopoeia'.[22]

In a play which focuses a good deal of attention on the nuts and bolts of its own art, the rehearsals of *Pyramus and Thisbe* rank amongst the most memorable moments. In fact, *A Midsummer Night's Dream*'s emphasis on 'playing' and on witnessing and giving audience in the broadest sense seems to acquire a palpable social bearing largely as a result of the complex connection between the fictions of drama and the nature of social reality so acutely probed by the mechanicals in those scenes. Their naïve and heavy-handed manipulation of established dramatic conventions serves, in effect, to make manifest the complex nature of the relationship between performer and audience, player and part, that drama brings about in any community. This, surely, is the serious point animating Bottom's famous injunction about naming:

> Nay, you must name his name, and half his face must be seen through the lion's neck; and he must himself speak through, saying thus, or to the same defect: 'Ladies', or 'Fair ladies, I would wish you,' or 'I would request you,' or 'I would entreat you, not to fear, not to tremble: my life for yours! If you think I come hither as a lion, it were pity of my life. No, I am no such thing; I am a man, as other men are': and there, indeed, let him name his name, and tell them plainly he is Snug the joiner.
>
> (III, i, 35ff.)

The essence of that relationship lies less in its capacity to afford entertainment or distraction from material social reality, than in the reverse: its capacity to confirm and reinforce the complexities of the social fabric. For to be 'a man as other men are' involves, in this setting, commitment to a *social* role over and above one's temporary, liberating carnival or festival role in a play. And it is this continuing social role that, in an oral community, finally imprints itself upon its bearer in the form of a name. Naming that name reinforces that role daily, branding its bearer on the tongue. One is plainly and manifestly understood to be Snug the Joiner, Bottom the Weaver, Quince the Carpenter, Snout the Tinker, Starveling the Tailor, or one is nothing, and the pages of names such as Joiner, Weaver, Carpenter, Tinker and Taylor, to say nothing of Wheelwright, Hunter or Smith still to be found in the telephone directories of modern Britain testify to the ubiquity of the practice.

Commitment to and involvement in an oral community is of course signalled and confirmed directly by the use of trade names in this fashion. In the cyclical structures characteristic of such societies, names and nature, speech and way of life, personal identity and social identity develop intricate links that the culture seeks to nourish and conserve. John of Gaunt's embodiment of the same ancient principle – he is Gaunt by name and gaunt by nature – proves memorably emblematic of a whole way of life under threat in *Richard II*.

That one's inherited and unchanging social role, imprinted in the utterance of one's very name, provides the solid basis for any temporary carnivalesque abandonment of that role, must be a first principle of a society whose way of life is fundamentally oral in mode. Everyone must know, by means of talking and listening, face to face, exactly who everyone else 'really' is. The temporary abandonment of that quotidian identity should not diminish, indeed it ought to strengthen, reinforce, even guarantee that social role.

The rehearsals for *Pyramus and Thisbe* make exactly this point and in these terms. The names of the characters are stressed from the beginning. The 'scroll of every man's name' (I, ii, 4) is presented, followed by the reading out of the 'names of the actors' and their trades in a careful ritual which covers the whole cast:

> *Quince*: Answer as I call you. Nick Bottom, the weaver?
> *Bottom*: Ready. Name what part I am for, and proceed.
>
> . . . .
> *Quince*: Francis Flute, the bellows-mender?
> *Flute*: Here, Peter Quince.
>
> (I, ii, 16ff.)

In both *Pyramus and Thisbe* and the framing play of *A Midsummer Night's Dream*, naming stands as an important, governing idea. The names of Titania's fairies, Peaseblossom, Cobweb, Moth (or Mote), Mustardseed, etc. are, of course, rootedly English. Moreover, Bottom assumes that their names and nature are indissolubly linked:

> I shall desire you of more acquaintance, good Master Cobweb: if I cut my finger, I shall make bold with you. . . . Good Master Mustardseed, I know your patience well. That same cowardly giant-like ox-beef hath devoured many a gentleman of your house: I promise you, your kindred hath made my eyes water ere now.
>
> (III, i, 175ff.)

In the case of Oberon's sprite, no single name proves adequate to his nature, so that the essentially English nomenclature expands to include 'Robin Goodfellow', 'Hobgoblin' and 'sweet Puck'(II, i, 34ff.)

– the merest gestures toward the plethora of names in which such creatures traditionally gloried. Reginald Scot's *The Discoverie of Witchcraft* (1584) records that

> Our mothers' maids have . . . so fraied us with bull beggars, spirits, witches, urchins, elves, hags, fairies, satyrs, Pans, fauns, sylens, Kit-with-the-Canstick, Tritons, centaurs, dwarfs, giants, imps, calcars, conjurors, nymphs, changelings, Incubus, Robin Goodfellow, the spoorne, the Mare, the Man in the Oak, the Hell wain, the Firedrake, the Puckle, Tom Thumb, Hobgoblin, Tom Tumbler, Boneless, and other such bugs, that we are afraid of our own shadows.[23]

The sheer number of these names records a commitment to precision and absolute aptness in the matter of nomenclature. Names conceived thus are obviously deeply resistant to change. When Wall announces

> In this same interlude it doth befall
> That I, one Snout by name, present a wall
> (V, i, 155)

and the Lion tells us

> Then know that I as Snug the joiner am
> A lion fell, nor else no lion's dam;
> For if I should as lion come in strife
> Into this place, 'twere pity on my life.
> (V, i, 218–21)

the amateur actors are reinforcing this important principle. Bottom – despite his transformation – is supposed to remain, at bottom, the fundamental self his name proclaims. Indeed, the process of joining or weaving together carnival role and social role, actor and audience, stage and auditorium could stand as the ultimate 'marriage' that the play aims to celebrate. Perhaps the physical structure of theatres like The Globe seemed, in their 'embracing' of their audiences, to propose and foster such a union. James Burbage, father of the actor Richard Burbage and the first builder of public playhouses, was a joiner by trade.

Yet change will not finally be warded off. All these named, rooted persons nevertheless undergo a kind of metamorphosis into the characters they play in *Pyramus and Thisbe*, and one of them, Bottom, suffers the most fundamental metamorphosis of all. Of course, they also remain the same. If there is any humour in Bottom's translation, it lies in the fact that, to some extent, he remains Bottom in spite of it. Yet their experience of 'or' springs out of their commitment to 'and'. Their names may give their essence, but their essence, paradoxically and inexplicably, somehow seems subject to change.

To return for the moment to the name with which we began: Nedar. At first sight the character seems simply an 'and', a repetition of the function of Egeus. But the fact that Nedar never appears on stage leaves a serious dimension of the matter open. And a Nedar indeterminate, unfixed, a potential 'or', remains a loose cannon careening dangerously across the play's deck. In truth, 'Nedar' engages with and fundamentally challenges the principle that names guarantee some kind of permanence and are resistant to change. If it were an anagram, the name would inevitably manifest an imperative for change (it would even propose a change from English to Greek) whilst at the same time – also as an anagram – it would disconcertingly assert a claim to remain the same. An anagram's fate is to embody the difference that repetition generates, to hint at 'or' beneath the surface of 'and', to live stretched between the tensions of contrary readings. *Nedar.* It is as if it aimed to disfigure 'and' altogether.

Wall

We owe to Brecht the observation that bad acting has considerable value in that it affords insights into the workings of drama itself.[24] That certainly proves to be the case with the performance of *Pyramus and Thisbe.* Its capacity for constant penetrative impingement on the 'main' narrative comes partly from its illuminating mimicry in miniature of the framing play's characteristic modes such as, here, in Peter Quince's disastrous performance, its hesitant, hiccuping circularity.

> If we offend, it is with our good will.
> That you should think, we come not to offend,
> But with good will. To show our simple skill,
> That is the true beginning of our end.
> Consider then, we come but in despite.
> (V, i, 108–12)

Nevertheless, *Pyramus and Thisbe* offers more than a mere caricature or travesty of aspects of *A Midsummer Night's Dream.* In effect, a wholesale revisionary and revealing re-reading takes place, in the course of which certain crucial changes of emphasis occur; and the use to which these are put indicates the extent to which the 'embedded' text aims to 'mean by' the drama which hosts it. Most clearly, *Pyramus and Thisbe* intensifies the enclosing play's concern with transgression. Of course, transgression is in any case a clearly signalled theme of *A Midsummer Night's Dream*. Bottom, a mere weaver, crosses massive social boundaries to become a version of the heroic lover. In his role as an ass, at the lower end of creation, he 'marries' Titania the fairy princess at the higher end. Acting, or role-playing, has always contained an obvious potential for trans-gression, particularly in a society regulated by rigid social hier-archies. But *Pyramus and Thisbe*'s foregrounding of role-playing throughout, particularly in the rehearsal scenes, positively trumpets its concern with the issue, something which the performance promises to reinforce when we hear it characterized in terms which themselves cross fundamental boundaries: it is 'hot ice', 'merry and tragical . . . tedious and brief' (V, i, 55ff.).

As a kind of monument to transgression, *Pyramus and Thisbe* seems appropriately enough to be constructed wholly and uniquely under the aegis of 'or'. From its very first appearance in Ovid, to its most famous representation in this play, its story is only ever told after the consideration of alternatives. In the *Metamorphoses* we hear that one of the daughters of Minyas 'knew a great many stories, so she considered which of them she ought to tell . . . she hesitated as to whether it should be the tale of Dercetis of Babylon who . . . was changed into a fish. . . . Finally she chose this last, for it was a little known tale.'[25] In *A Midsummer Night's Dream*, Theseus is invited to choose between 'The Battle with the Centaurs' or 'The riot of the tipsy Bacchanals' or 'The thrice three Muses mourning' before settling on *Pyramus and Thisbe*. Permanently commutable, 'or' haunts even the glimpses we see of the play in rehearsal. Indeed rehearsal, with its testing out of alternatives, is the dramatic mode which 'or' most comfortably inhabits.

Acts of transgression not only cross boundaries, they also reveal them, and *Pyramus and Thisbe*'s literal-minded presentation of a fundamental boundary on the stage, and the clear intention of the mechanicals to make meaning from it, constitutes a memorable and telling statement. In the absence of the fathers (or mothers) of the enclosing play, the restrictive devices which keep the lovers apart here find themselves materially represented by a wall (played, curiously, by Snout, who was originally cast to play Pyramus's father) aided and abetted by a moon (played by Starveling, originally cast as Thisbe's mother).

Walls traditionally support, separate and thus preserve by division. A wall both recognizes difference and proposes its maintenance: it is a bulwark against change. Since we are here dealing with speaking walls, we might say that a wall, with its commitment to conservation, to more of the same, characteristically says 'and'.

All societies make use of walls, literally or metaphorically deployed, and they obviously supply a major means of generating and reinforcing meaning in any culture. To breach a wall, or to transgress the boundary it marks, risks challenging the structure of differences on which meaning in a society is based. To breach or transgress a wall is to say 'or'.

It follows that the paradox of a wall *intended* for breaching must generate a fundamental contradiction. It will say 'or' as well as 'and'. Yet, of course, such contradictions undoubtedly exist although the aim of any discourse will normally be to occlude them. A good example of the paradox of the wall expressly intended for breaching occurs in respect of female sexuality. Obviously a number of symbolic 'walls' surround the virgin female. Yet these must be breached in order that licensed procreation may take place and the culture persist. Virginity itself, and indeed the physical hymen, appears not infrequently in Elizabethan writing as a 'wall' which the male marriage partner/lover must breach, but in circumstances carefully controlled and approved by law and custom. This generates the contradictions in which the rite of passage marked by loss of virginity is shrouded: 'legitimate' violation, 'cohesive' breaching, an 'authorized' transgression, an act of physical violence undertaken as an ultimate act of gentle responsiveness, the drawing of blood in the name of love.

Pyramus and Thisbe's Wall, which aids and abets its own breaching, clearly foregrounds the issue of boundaries and their transgression, and in so doing serves to highlight particular aspects of the framing play. The contradictions linking violence and affection, from Egeus's threat to 'disfigure' his daughter, to those surrounding sexual defloration, abound. The idea of 'wooing' with a sword, of 'winning love' through 'doing injuries' (I, i, 16–17) proliferates from the beginning of *A Midsummer Night's Dream*. 'Wounding' in the name of love is symbolized in Oberon's account of 'Cupid's fiery shaft' which penetrates the 'little western flower,/Before milk-white, now purple with love's wound' (II, i, 166–7). That, in turn, becomes the source of the love-juice which sparks the plot. In Montrose's words, 'the imagery of the text insinuates that . . . Oberon's maddening love-juice is a displacement of vaginal blood'.[26] The story of *Pyramus and*

Thisbe in its turn insists on and reinforces the same motif with its spectacularly symbolic bloody ending (as well as in Pyramus's encounter with Thisbe's bloodstained mantle and, in this production, Bottom's malapropian conclusion that 'lion vile hath here deflower'd my dear' (V, i, 281)). Presented to a society as fundamentally conservative as Theseus's Athens, however, even a 'courteous' and obliging Wall involves a challenge to respectability which may risk the penalty of hanging. The problem is that however much the players' anxiety and consequent stratagems try to avoid such a confrontation, it seems built in to the very medium in which they now find themselves involved.

Steven Mullaney's work effectively defines the role of the Elizabethan theatre in terms of walls and its relationship to them.[27] The theatre's place and status were marginal and ambiguous precisely because it was situated outside the City's walls, within the ambivalent area known as the 'licentious Liberties'. The ambiguous role of the players ('doble-dealing ambodexters') is confirmed by the contradictory allegiances and functions of the theatres. Neither within nor without the city, irregular and uncertain in their standing, they existed 'where the powers of city, state and church came together but did not coincide'.[28] By 1599 the city was ringed with playhouses, but the flight of the theatres from the city centre to its margins demanded to be seen metaphorically as a flight to liberty, not banishment.

The notion of margin, as Mullaney points out, proposes an appropriate metaphor in that it refers to an indeterminate space used for commentary on a main text, a commentary whose arguments inevitably challenge and threaten to become part of that text and even to submerge it. In social terms, the theatre certainly seemed capable of undermining the imaginary wall dividing 'margin' from 'main text'. Worse, its refusal of that polarity's stability threatened to bring other defining walls and boundaries within the society into crisis. As we have seen, the theatre also breached the wall separating audience from performer. And as *Pyramus and Thisbe* confirms, it persistently encouraged those engaged with it to become participants in a social context that wished them to remain spectators.

What the city feared from the theatre was precisely the political dimension of this impulse towards participation. After all, the theatres were places where unemployed and unemployable 'masterless men' might 'recreate themselves'.[29] The extra-mural status of the theatre, its embodiment of the idea of a limit or 'Liberty' confronting and challenging social restraint, confirms the capacity of this kind of drama to question the structure of commonsense which the city endorses. By definition, the margin is where authority faces its own limits. Characteristically, the very existence of those restricted to a periphery will inevitably bring the fundamental, meaning-making status of the centre into question. The periphery's role is to be the abode of the threatening 'other' by which the centre's 'norm' can be defined.[30] But it is no mere lair. In fact, it offers a unique vantage point from which the process of 'meaning by', as this operates at the centre, can be observed. As a result, possible alternative processes can be plotted and different meanings conceived from there. Its 'otherness' characterizes precisely the nature of the challenge it inevitably makes. The periphery, the margin, is the position from which, in the terms I have been using, the theatres might be said to scream 'or' in the face of the city's 'and'.

Author! Author!

One could hardly expect Bottom and his troupe to be wholly sensitive to the critical revisionary role in which this seems to cast them. Yet there is a palpable edge to their humility, an exhilarating sense that their play has the power to disconcert as well as entertain, that a heady potential for 'offence' lies, for once, near to hand. The performance of *Pyramus and Thisbe* is not quite the comfortable and comforting occasion that some readings try to make it.[31] In a similar case, my own words composed for Nedar, claiming to speak in the play's name, might seem to assert, from the margin or the periphery, a malapert equality with the Bard at the centre that is not quite laughable enough. To write the poet's words for him! To leap, at one bound, the wall separating commentary from creativity! For a literary critic, as for a rude mechanical, this is a part to tear a cat in, to make all split! In some eyes, it might also bear an uncomfortable resemblance to the sin against the Holy Ghost.

In mitigation, I will plead that I am only making overt and raising to a slightly higher power a process which, in literary criticism, is usually covert and gently occluded. Foucault cites commentary on texts as a major 'internal' system of cultural exclusion and limitation whereby discourses are established and confirmed, restricted and focused.[32] Most commentary – at least in the Anglo-American academy – certainly ends by building a kind of wall around the texts it deals with, one which aims to define the work by containing it. It performs a policing action whose *modus operandi* almost literally involves a kind of repetition. For criticism's fundamental mode, as perceived at large in Britain and North America, is indeed that of retelling the text's story for it, of rewriting the poet's words on his or her behalf, of re-presenting the work of literature as it supposedly fully, and finally is, with all its contradictions, silences and ambiguities finally teased out, realized, resolved, and cemented into place. Institutions and syllabuses supply moat and fortification. It is a way of saying 'and'.

There are many aspects of *A Midsummer Night's Dream* which lead finally to the topic of literary criticism. Not least is the way in which the obligations and responsibilities of filiation, the problematic relationships between parents and children with which the play begins, are ultimately and emblematically repeated, re-presented and resolved through the agency of larger social relationships, or affiliations, and the concomitant activity I have called 'meaning by'. In other words, in the presentation of *Pyramus and Thisbe*, the filiative bonds and duties agitating Egeus, Hermia, Helena and the rest find themselves recuperated in the transactions of a specific social grouping, that of the 'rude mechanicals'. Whatever its potential, their comic performance effectively re-reads and redeploys the narrative, managing to drain the tragedy away without seriously undermining the practices that caused it. Edward Said cites this transition from a 'failed idea or possibility of filiation' to a kind of compensatory social order, or affiliation, as a central feature of our cultural experience:

> if a filial relationship was held together by natural bonds and natural forms of authority – involving obedience, fear, love, respect and instinctual conflict – the new affiliative relationship changes these bonds into what seem to be transpersonal forms – such as guild consciousness, consensus, collegiality, professional respect, class, and the hegemony of a dominant culture.[33]

What the performance of *Pyramus and Thisbe* seems to indicate is that the affiliations developed in the business of 'making meaning' in society offer a way, by means of repetition and re-presentation, of dealing with issues that are otherwise apparently intractable. In short, the efforts of the mechanicals to 'mean by' *Pyramus and Thisbe* reformulate and reassemble problems on behalf of and for the benefit of a community that overtly mocks, yet covertly gains reassurance from the procedure. This process – it is one of containment – can be seen as a kind of acculturation, one which it is often considered to be the business of the academic literary critic to promote and authenticate. On this basis, Said concludes that the relationship between filiation and affiliation can be said to lie 'located at the heart of critical consciousness'.[34]

Certainly within the academy – that very model of affiliation – criticism's role is often thought to involve smoothing the journey from one condition to the other. Indeed, the herding of texts within the academy's affiliative structures and the branding of them as approved cultural products has often been taken as the major function of the academic literary critic. It is a process which, in requiring the text to be appropriately dissected and redeployed, domesticated and tamed, has seemed to make the academic critic an inveterate promoter of 'and'.

Theseus would certainly approve of that function. His project, speaking for the audience of *Pyramus and Thisbe*, clearly involves sifting and realigning the mechanicals' performance in order to discover a preferred meaning in it. Invited by Philostrate to 'find sport in their intents' (V, i, 79) he confirms that, in respect of the mechanicals' text, 'Our sport shall be to take what they mistake' (V, i, 90) and he goes on to elaborate a miniature theory of critical reading whose procedures can effectively police any public text. His examples prefigure exactly what happens in the case of *Pyramus and Thisbe*:

> Where I have come, great clerks have purposed
> To greet me with premeditated welcomes;
> Where I have seen them shiver and look pale,
> Make periods in the midst of sentences,
> Throttle their practis'd accent in their fears,
> And, in conclusion, dumbly have broke off,
> Not paying me a welcome. Trust me, sweet,
> Out of this silence yet I pick'd a welcome,
> And in the modesty of fearful duty
> I read as much as from the rattling tongue
> Of saucy and audacious eloquence.
>
> (V, i, 90ff.)

The grounding procedure recommended here is one of picking out, and painfully isolating and reassembling the units of a preferred version of a text. Applied to reading, it presents that activity as a selective, shaping and revising redeployment, a carefully moderated process of 'meaning by' which offers to speak for the text, to 'repeat' what it says, to insist on its behalf that the text does say certain things, to allow that it also says a possible range of other things, but no more. Usually, the interpretation focuses on contradictions, which it smoothes over, ambiguities, which it disentangles and limits, and silences which it confirms, accounts for, or which it makes to speak in accordance with what has been recognized as an overriding point of view. Critical reading thus conceived threads its way between two extremes: on the one hand, that represented by Borges's creation Pierre Menard, whose *Don Quixote* repeats every word of Cervantes's text as these occur on the page but by that very act claims to generate a wholly new text; and on the other hand, a commentary which produces new words that the text does not contain, but which can be said to present and reinforce its essential meaning more rigorously than those supplied by its first author.

My words for Nedar would seem to fall into this latter category. Thus my bringing of this silent character to the point of speech could be said to be not so much impudent or sacrilegious as to involve the implementation of the first principle of one kind of literary criticism: to present a confirming and, since I write as an academic literary critic, an affiliating repetition which aims to function as an act of containment, a beating of intellectual bounds which is also the beating of a tribal drum.

If that is so, then, to redirect one of the arguments outlined above, *Pyramus and Thisbe* can be permitted no 'essential' quality which would guarantee a consistent commitment to 'or'. Theseus's re-deploying shadow (no less than my own) falls across all claims as to its function. Read in a particular way, perhaps as Theseus proposes to do, it could just as easily be made to say 'and'. At the very most, Theseus's speech and my words for Nedar could be said to exemplify a principle whereby 'and' is enabled to disguise itself as 'or'. And this is confirmed if all commentary can in any case, by Foucault's limiting definition, only be of the sort that 'allows us to say something other than the text itself, but on condition that it is this text itself which is said, and in a sense completed'.[35]

We might add to that assessment an earlier one made by Hazlitt which is – from one point of view – no less disconcerting on the subject of literary texts. Writing of *Coriolanus*, he points to what he sees as poetry's final complicity with the social forces that it sets out to question. The language of poetry, he claims, 'naturally falls in with the language of power' on the grounds that it springs not from the understanding, ' a distributive faculty which seeks the greatest quantity of ultimate good, by justice and proportion', but from the imagination, 'a monopolising faculty, which seeks the greatest quantity of present excitement by inequality and disproportion'.[36] The American critic Lionel Trilling would certainly agree. Poetry's 'affinity with political power', he writes, makes it 'not a friend of the democratic virtues'.[37] Elizabethan poetic drama's apparent collusion with conservative political positions has often seemed to mark it as inimical to change – something seized on by the eighteenth-century radical John Thelwall when he argued that it was precisely because the Puritans were 'friends of liberty' that they despised the theatre.[38] By this light, everything says 'and', nothing says 'or'. It is a cheerless picture.

Mr Asquith's smile

On 6 February 1914, the figure of Nedar actually trod the English stage. Harley Granville-Barker's 'golden' production of the play brought what he evidently read as Helena's father into the final act where, speechless, he brought symmetry to the grouping around the performance of *Pyramus and Thisbe*.

It was a production which took place at one of the most crucial moments in British cultural history. The First World War was only months away. Industrial unrest was rapidly burgeoning: between January and July 1914 no fewer than 937 strikes took place. A General Strike, based on the Triple Alliance, loomed. A massive rebellion – almost a revolution – seemed on the cards in Northern Ireland. By March, a mutiny among officers at the Curragh garrison there had ushered in what George Dangerfield calls 'a new and terrible England'.[39] And yet there was a further factor which, by the time Parliament opened on 10 February, could be seen to have more revolutionary implications than any of these. Like *A Midsummer Night's Dream*, it focused centrally upon the rights of women.

The Suffragette movement can in many respects be credited with the initiation of modern militant street politics involving organized and violent protest. Its outrageous campaign of bombs, wire-severing, window-smashing, picture-slashing, heckling, hunger-strikes, invasion of political meetings, sit-down protests and the like had been met by remedies that now seem familiar: imprisonment, pulpit denunciation, endless prevarication and, an appalling specific, the use of the dreaded feeding tube.

Yet matters were obviously reaching a climax. Suffragette arson was to set no less than 107 buildings on fire during the first seven months of 1914. Mrs Pankhurst had already endured several hunger strikes, and between 9 March and 18 July of that year was to raise her record of such experiences to ten. By now, says George Dangerfield, 'her appearance was terrifying'.[40] Royalty had become involved. In June of the previous year, Emily Wilding Davison had made the supreme sacrifice for the cause and thrown herself under the hooves of the King's horse at the Derby.

The theatre naturally offered an irresistible arena, particularly if royalty could be involved. In December 1913, at a gala performance at Covent Garden of Raymond Roze's opera *Jeanne d'Arc* given in the presence of the King and Queen, some suffragettes secretly barricaded themselves in a box directly opposite the monarch's, stood up at the close of the first Act and, using a megaphone, addressed their Majesties forcefully. They were at pains to draw parallels between nature and art: between the women's struggle outside the theatre and Joan of Arc's fight for liberty in the face of torture and death within it. When they were ejected, forty or more other women in the audience waited until the performance had begun again before raining suffragist literature down onto the outraged spectators.[41] On another occasion, the King found himself confronted by a woman who had chained herself to a seat in the stalls at a matinée at His Majesty's Theatre, in order to denounce him loudly as 'You Russian Tsar!'[42] By 1914 the public protests were drawing even nearer. At a Drawing Room in that year, May Blomfield fell dramatically to her knees before the royal couple crying 'For God's Sake, Your Majesty, put a stop to this forcible feeding!'[43]

The Royal Presence, as reports had it, 'remained serene' but the theatricality of such protests must, by 1914, have given its advisers pause.[44] Did they, we may wonder, have any qualms over their Majesties' proposed visit to the Granville-Barker production of *A Midsummer Night's Dream*, with its pivotal scene in which Hermia is reminded of the duties a daughter owes to her father?

Granville-Barker's production characteristically sought very firmly to link the present to what he perceived as the realities of a Shakespearean past in which nothing was to be spared. The fairies were given a bizarre and slightly threatening mien that deliberately challenged traditional preconceptions involving small children swathed in tulle. The music of Mendelssohn was firmly banished in favour of traditional English airs set by Cecil Sharp.

Symmetry at many levels was a feature of the production and that is usually seen as the basis for the inclusion in the company of Nedar, as Helena's father. Helena was played by the famous actress Lillah McCarthy, co-producer of the scintillating Savoy Shakespeare productions and at that time also Granville-Barker's wife, although the marriage was by then under some strain. They began to live apart from 1916 onwards and divorced two years later. In an oddly vacuous account of her life, Lillah McCarthy refers to this as 'the most beautiful production of my career' – principally, it appears, because of the golden wig she wore, which apparently made the audience – and the King and Queen when they came – 'love' her.[45]

No doubt they did. A golden wig has immeasurable power. Nevertheless, six years before, on Sunday, 21 June 1908, a possibly less immediately lovable Lillah McCarthy had ridden as one notable amongst others at the very head of a procession organized by The Women's Social and Political Union to Hyde Park, where 250,000 suffragettes had gathered.[46] The *Daily Express* said of the occasion, 'It is probable that so many people never before stood in one square mass anywhere in England.'[47]

As Lillah McCarthy later put it, 'We were all suffragettes in those days. . . . I had walked in processions. I had carried banners for Mrs. Pankhurst and the Cause'.[48] Indeed, she had done more. Her autobiography tells of a particular occasion, 'a year or two before the war' when, finding herself briefly alone in the Cabinet Room of Number 10 Downing Street, she boldly wrote 'Votes for Women' in red grease paint across the blotting paper on the Prime Minister's desk. 'When the rehearsal for which I had gone to Downing Street was over, Mr. Asquith came to me. We had tea together. He asked: "Why do you think women should have the vote?" By Heaven I told him! I poured out arguments in no unstinted measure. He greeted them with a quizzical smile.'[49]

It is a moment to savour. Mr Asquith's smile, capable of dissolving the theatre's revolutionary potential represented by that intrusive red grease-paint, lingers across the years until it acquires almost symbolic status as a characteristic British way of deflecting social upheaval: silent (and in this case male) reproof. Possibly, it even glimmers faintly within Granville-Barker's production of *A Midsummer Night's Dream,* as if Asquith had suddenly found himself translated into the silent male Nedar, there to curb the potential upheaval that, like an unruly daughter, Lillah McCarthy might so easily have injected into the role of Helena. We can be quite precise about the context. In London, in 1914, one toss of that golden wig could have made the character shriek 'Votes for Women'. The slightest vocal inflection might have externalized the production's potential for 'or'. Of course, nothing of the kind took place.

To say that this is what Granville-Barker intended is perhaps to propose a significance for silence that the occasion hardly warrants. Nevertheless, it seems reasonable to suggest that quiescence in such matters was not merely desirable, but as much part of what was 'meant by' the production as the determined 'Englishness' of Cecil

Sharp's music (which silenced Mendelssohn) and the menacing fairies (which suppressed grassy banks and tulle). Given the play's and the occasion's potential, as I have tried to sketch these, it was a silence which spoke.

When Lillah McCarthy came to write her account of these years, a similar soundless fatherly male presence continued to supervene. By the gambit of legally forbidding any mention of his own name in her reminiscences (he is referred to only obliquely, for example, as 'the producer'), Granville-Barker's absence generated a tacit, rebuking presence there too.[50] His mute male Nedar had been eloquent on his behalf in 1914. Under the producer's on-going surveillance, subsequent texts were to remain evidently (albeit paradoxically) unproductive, permitted only to say 'and'.

Round or round the mulberry bush

Must all readings, all performances, fail to release the 'or' for which 'and' creates the potential? History suggests that Liberty needs more effective friends than Mr Asquith. And Hazlitt's view is a partial one. It mistakenly separates poetry from the response and analysis that always and everywhere accompany it. It is also a mistake to think of literary criticism as something subsequent to and dependent upon 'creative' writing. There is no writing without criticism, and the distinction between them is surely misleading. There are few 'creative' writers (Hazlitt amongst them) who are not also critics. All writers are critical readers of writing, even if their reading is limited to their own work. In other words, it is vital to resist the simple dismissal of criticism as necessarily parasitic. The presentation of critics as mere lice on the locks of literature saves the face of too many third-rate writers, as Oscar Wilde knew.[51] And the division between 'creative' writer and critic confirms too many ideological contours to be taken at face value.

Also, as I have argued above, no commentary can simply repeat the text in its own terms, or lay claim to the discovery of its once-for-all 'meaning'. No criticism can simply dance around and around the same mulberry bush. All criticism – whether it intends to or not – effectively creates a potential space for 'or': there is no escape from metamorphosis, and the study of the process by which critical analysis systematically converts literature to its own purposes could even become, as I have suggested elsewhere, the basis of a new notion of the subject 'English', and so the means of breaking asunder the affiliation whose conservative mode both Said and Foucault deplore.[52]

A critical stance which self-consciously seeks to raise this process to the highest power, to embrace its implications rather than occlude them, must thus have a high priority. The method of such a commentary would, of necessity, be to refuse absolutely to encounter the text on its own terms, to refuse the text's own hierarchy of character and event, and to read and re-read it seeking out what it suppresses, marginalizes and silences as part of its own project.

Marx could be said to have made these stratagems the basis of a powerful method of historical analysis. Its *locus classicus* occurs in his *The Eighteenth Brumaire of Louis Bonaparte*, an account of Louis Napoleon's coup of December 1851, in which a savage 'replaying' of events and a mordantly satirical retelling of a particular narrative becomes the central concern. Marx begins by citing Hegel's view that 'all facts and personages of great importance in world history occur, as it were, twice'. But he points out – interestingly from the point of view of the performance of *Pyramus and Thisbe* – that Hegel forgot to add that what occurs the first time as tragedy, takes place the second time as farce. The force of Marx's formulation lies in its energetic grasp of the power for change this offers to the reteller of the story. His aim is to depict the 1851 coup as a farcical repetition of its predecessors in circumstances 'that made it possible for a grotesque mediocrity to play a hero's part'.[53] And it is precisely Marx's recapitulation of the events, particularly from 1848 to 1851, his redescription, and his careful replay of a complex series of developments and relationships, that demonstrate his point, produce and justify the polemic, and show 'meaning by' in the process of taking place. The *Eighteenth Brumaire* is thus, as Edward Said has argued, an exemplary text for literary critics: its method 'to repeat in order to produce difference', its mode an 'and' designed to produce 'or'.[54]

Herein lies whatever significance may be claimed for the words I have immodestly invented for Nedar: they say 'and' in order to generate 'or'. It is of course vital that they turn the character into a woman, Helena's mother. That simple step, that repetition which is also a re-reading and a redeployment of something apparently 'obvious' in the text, makes all the difference. Indeed, it makes meaningful difference possible, and the issues at stake in 'meaning by' the play overt and unavoidable. It does so, not because Nedar necessarily *is* female, but because, in twentieth-century terms, the suggestion that she could be unseats a number of presuppositions investing the play and demonstrates an indeterminacy, an undecidability, that is a feature of all texts. Any 'resolution' of that indeterminacy will generate a coherent reading, but it will of course be one haunted by the alternatives that its own existence has perforce suppressed. It will be a reading aware of, and embodying, its own potential status as an 'or' rather than an 'and'. Given that, Nedar's words may 'repeat' the text, but at the same time, to flatter both myself and them, they also offer to present it for the first time.

Pyramus and Thisbe, the repetition as farce of the near-tragedy of *A Midsummer Night's Dream*, yields a potent symbol of the lovers' transgression: the blood-darkened mulberry tree. Human history has a way of imposing its own metamorphoses even on fictional events – in this case by its domestication of the mulberry tree and the metaphorical draining away of its bloody import, so that the colour of its leaves no longer hints at death or defloration. But oddly enough, the story of the metamorphosis of the mulberry tree finally has a rather precise and reassuringly farcical connection with Shakespeare. Legend has it that when he bought New Place in Stratford-upon-Avon, within a year or so of writing *A Midsummer Night's Dream*, the Bard planted a mulberry tree in its Great Garden. By the eighteenth century, the great increase in his fame had caused seekers after mementoes to pester the then owner of New Place, the Rev. Francis Gastrell, to such a degree that in 1758 he ordered the tree cut down. It was then sold to a Mr Thomas Sharpe, a watchmaker, who proceeded over the next forty years to bring about a rather more mundane, but no less effective metamorphosis by carving the remnants into hundreds of tiny objects – far more, it was said, than a single tree could genuinely yield – and selling them to visitors and tourists at great profit.[55]

Their appeal is understandable. Some sort of organic link with the imagined past continues to be one of the central fantasies of modern society. Shadowy yearnings for an originary, pastoral root from which we can be said to spring, are considerable, formative agencies. They have sparked many a grassy, rabbit-ridden production of *A Midsummer Night's Dream*. An 'original' growth from Shakespeare's Garden! Planted by the Bard's Hand! Like other wooden structures – the Birthplace, Anne Hathaway's Cottage, the Original Globe Theatre – the mulberry tree seems to offer a continually self-renewing 'and', one which nature in this case seems, in the very rotation of the seasons, always to confirm.

In fact, such are the needs of the twentieth century that present-day visitors to Shakespeare's garden find themselves in the presence not of one, but of two mulberry trees. The first and larger specimen lays stress on its filiation by announcing itself to be 'a scion of the tree planted by Shakespeare near his last residence'. The second, smaller tree confirms its filiative status as an 'offspring of the parent tree nearby', but then, proclaiming its planting 'by Dame Peggy Ashcroft, 8th September 1969' moves almost predictably into the sphere of affiliation by recording its commemoration of the two hundredth anniversary of the first Shakespeare Festival organized by David Garrick in 1769. Both trees seem to proclaim 'and', the second even adding an 'and' to the first. The issues addressed by *A Midsummer Night's Dream* could find no better memorial.

But if we needed a subtler emblem for the use of criticism in our society, the industrious Mr Sharpe – unsung final heir to the Pyramus and Thisbe legend – has perhaps genuinely whittled it for us. In producing an endless series of different objects carved from the same source, and indeed outstripping that source's material capacity to supply and sustain them, he is an apt figure for the literary critic, generating 'or's which masquerade as 'and's, flagrantly making and remaking whatever the text might be said once to have meant in order the better to 'mean by' it now. We can only, in the spirit proposed by the mechanicals of *A Midsummer Night's Dream*, urge that such a figure should shamelessly and fully embrace the implications of its function: name his name, in short, and announce boldly that he is Sharpe the Watchmaker. We know that to be no final bulwark against the onslaught of time. But at the very least, as Peter Quince promised, its bearer might escape hanging.

3 Shakespeare and the General Strike

Our England is a garden that is full of stately views,
Of borders, beds and shrubberies and lawns and avenues,
With statues on the terraces and peacocks strutting by;
But the Glory of the Garden lies in more than meets the eye.
(Kipling, *The Glory of the Garden*)

Criticism on strike

There is a particular statue in the centre of the city of Cardiff whose inscription has always seemed to me to offer a text suitable for the most stringent critical analysis. Its six words are pithy and pointed. 'John Cory', it says, 'Coal-Owner and Philanthropist'.

Any person memorialized in such a fashion must surely have been a connoisseur of the oxymoron. I hope that the similarly opposed polarities of the present essay's title would have appealed to him. For both texts, as befits their South Wales provenance, are rooted in coal, and the concerns of mine are apparently no less contradictory than those of his. After all, 'Shakespeare and the General Strike' links on the one hand Art (for which Shakespeare can stand as an appropriate symbol), something that in social terms may be said to be binding, bonding, and reinforcing; and on the other hand Politics, of which industrial action, or the strike, is an apt representative. The contradiction comes about because a strike, with the abruptness that the word suggests, represents an immediate refusal, an incisive severing of the social, political and economic bonds that supposedly bind human communities together.

Any strike is always an astonishing moment in human history. Suddenly, often violently, the event reaches beyond the polite, tacitly agreed, philanthropic surface of society to lay bare what some would call its real foundations. And in its brusque refusal of some of the basic assumptions of those foundations, the strike seems almost to threaten their dissolution. The term itself proposes fundamental disruption. It offers, in miniature, what Fredric Jameson calls 'the figure for social revolution'.[1]

So the title 'Shakespeare and the General Strike' presents a contradiction of a radical kind. Art and Politics, in our culture, are not just opposites, they rank as the organizing epicentres of two quite contrary discourses. Hence the sense of an unbreachable wall separating one from the other. Hence the outcry normally raised against the very idea of any conjunction, or any common ground. To propose that such a possibility exists is almost to sanction some illicit act of transgression in which a grubby 'Politics' may be 'dragged' across a threshold to sully the otherwise sacrosanct shrine of Art. Worse, reversing the process, Shakespeare himself might even be 'dragged into politics'.

Of course, the trap of essentialism lies in wait for the unwary critic here. 'Art', it can be said, has no necessary commitment to binding, bonding, affirmation. Any work can be *read* in an oppositional mode, or to a subversive purpose. Equally, a 'strike' often generates bonding amongst its participants: it can and does develop its own kind of affiliative unity. These are important considerations. However, my focus here is on ways in which the world is experienced and understood as meaningful in terms of the 'common sense' which all cultures habitually and uncritically endorse as the basis of existence. And Art – particularly the art of Shakespeare – is certainly understood by our society on that 'common-sense' level as wholly capable of unsullied transcendence over the everyday sphere of profit margins, market forces, redundancies and wage settlements. Strikes, on the same level, are deemed to be quintessentially of that world and in it. The separation seems absolute. But the central concern of this essay is not just to confirm that this is the way things appear to be. It also – in so doing – implies a challenge to and a questioning of that arrangement. Perhaps what it calls for is a strike against common sense.

Over the top

In fact, Shakespeare presents an immediate opportunity for that and in precisely those terms. Of all his plays, *Coriolanus* seems so regularly and so provocatively to connect with political events outside the text that it immediately offers to undermine the common-sense separation with which we began. The process has a long history, dating from the play's composition. Some scholars argue that it possibly bears some imprint of the riots of 1607–8 in the Midlands.[2] The fundamental opposition it constructs between patricians and plebeians, and the involvement in that of an arrogant and charismatic military hero whose final march to sack Rome is stayed only by the pleas of his mother, suggests links with various aspects of post-Renaissance class conflict.

Certainly, by the nineteenth and early twentieth centuries the play regularly seems to chafe against the boundaries of that 'Art' category to which common sense so earnestly wants to consign it. It has been noticed above that, long before the advent of New Historicism or Cultural Materialism, the radical eighteenth-century activist John Thelwall argued that the Elizabethan theatre was 'in reality a question of politics', both in its own day and subsequently. Right-wing critics took the point. William Hazlitt's disturbing essay on *Coriolanus*, already mentioned, was roundly condemned with the rest of his Shakespearean criticism as 'seditious' in 1817 by William Gifford, the most powerful London editor of the day, because it offered an example of what Jonathan Bate calls a 'new kind of political criticism'. Bate rightly places Hazlitt and Thelwall on one side and Coleridge on the other in what amounts to an ideological tussle for ownership of the National Poet.[3]

The process continued. In Charlotte Brontë's novel *Shirley* (1849), chapter VI is entitled 'Coriolanus'. Caroline Helstone and Robert Moore read the play together in the presence of his sister Hortense, as a way of passing an evening, and as a significant stage in their courtship. They proceed to discuss it against a clear background of political and industrial unrest: that of the novel's own plot (1811-12), and that of its actual composition (1848).

Robert, a mill-owner whose new frames have been destroyed by Luddite workers, admires and sympathizes with Coriolanus, but Caroline calls that a 'vicious point': 'you sympathise with that proud patrician who does not sympathise with his famished fellow-men and insults them'. Despite this 'brotherhood in error', she persuades him that, since Coriolanus's major sin was pride 'you must not be proud to your workpeople; you must not neglect chances of soothing them, and you must not be of an inflexible nature, uttering a request as austerely as if it were a command.' 'I never wish you to lower yourself', she continues, 'but somehow, I cannot help thinking it unjust to include all poor working people under the general and insulting name of "the mob" and continually to think of them and treat them haughtily.'[4]

March on Rome

In the twentieth century, Coriolanus's disdain of the mob connects intimately with anti-democratic developments in Europe after the First World War and further deepens the play's material involvement in the politics of everyday. Between December 1933 and February 1934, a production of René Louis Piachaud's version of *Coriolanus* at the Comédie-Française, sponsored by the right-wing party Action Française, sought to present it as a Fascist denunciation of democracy and provoked riots in the streets of Paris. School editions and performances of the play along similar lines were popular in Nazi Germany throughout the 1930s and *Coriolanus* was banned by occupying American forces when they reached Berlin in 1945.[5] A famous production planned by the Berliner Ensemble in 1962/3 proposed using Brecht's unfinished adaptation of the play to present it as a denunciation of Fascism in which the working classes, educated by their tribunes, rise to overthrow their patrician oppressors.[6] The ironies of that (in the light of previous developments in East Germany, in which an actual rising against the rigidities of Communist rule had occurred) were later explored and slightly fictionalized in Günter Grass's play *The Plebeians Rehearse the Uprising* (1966) which dwells specifically – if not incisively – on the complexity of the barrier between Art and Politics and the difficulties encountered by any attempt at transgression.[7]

In short, with the opposition between Art and Politics still our central concern, the twentieth century offers a number of opportunities for a yet narrower focus on the issue, and in pursuit of it, it might be helpful now to close in on a particular day in a particular year. Since our interest is with Shakespeare on the one hand and political/industrial action on the other, the coordinates to some extent choose themselves. Let the day be 23 April, Shakespeare's Birthday. Let the year be 1926, the occasion of the General Strike, one of the major political upheavals of modern times in Britain. And, for good measure, we can add an appropriately symbolic place: Stratford-upon-Avon, Shakespeare's Birthplace, right at the centre of England.

Of course, the period 1925 to 1926 was one of unprecedented political and social tension in Britain and it is worth trying to recall some of the details. So-called 'Red Friday', 31 July 1925, offers an appropriate point of departure. On that day, the Prime Minister, Stanley Baldwin, agreed to continue subsidizing the faltering coal-mining industry and thus to protect miners' wages. One of the reasons for what his enemies saw as a major retreat was the fear of civil strife: different political groups within the country were said to be spoiling for a fight, and in a report to the King, the Permanent Secretary to the Cabinet, Maurice Hankey, had claimed that 'Fascists numbering anything from fifty to a hundred thousand are organized for different reasons.'[8]

Fascists in Britain! The movement known as the British Fascists had been founded just two years previously, in 1923, by a young woman called Rotha Lintorn-Orman.[9] Initially known as the 'British Fascisti', they were incorporated in 1924 as a limited company, with the not overly bellicose title of 'British Fascists, Ltd.', their main object being to counter reiterated trade-union threats of industrial action by proposing schemes to 'maintain public order and guarantee essential services'.[10] The example of Mussolini was a potent one. His much-trumpeted, Coriolanus-like 'March on Rome' in 1922 had presented Fascism as the means of saving Italy from Bolshevism, and by 1926 those two terms were being used to nominate the polarities for political squaring-off in Britain at a popular level. The enrolment form for the British Fascists required an entrant to undertake to 'render every service in my power to the British Fascisti in their struggle against all treacherous and revolutionary movements now working for the destruction of the Throne and Empire', and conditions were certainly ripe for conflict at this slightly hysterical level.[11] On 2 August 1925, the Home Secretary, Sir William Joynson-Hicks, opined that 'Sooner or later this question has got to be fought out by the people of the land. Is England to be governed by Parliament and the Cabinet or by a handful of Trade Union leaders?'[12]

On 8 October 1925, at the annual conference of the Tory party at Brighton, Baldwin had promised to consider prosecuting the Communist Party. On 14 October 1925, Joynson-Hicks announced (at an evening performance of an amateur dramatic society) 'I believe that the greater part of the audience will be pleased to hear that warrants have been issued and in the majority of cases have been executed for the arrest of a certain number of notorious Communists.' There followed what one historian has called 'the first overtly political trial in England since the days of the Chartists'. Sentences of between six and twelve months imprisonment were imposed on a dozen people. By 24 October, George Lansbury, the Socialist leader, was asserting that the Communists were part of 'the indivisible movement of the working class'. Within days, more than two hundred South Wales miners were sentenced to terms of between fourteen days and twelve months for acts of violence during a strike in July.[13] No doubt, by now, even John Cory's philanthropy might have been feeling some slight strain.

Let us move into 1926. On 7 February of that year, the so-called 'Release the Prisoners Day', massive demonstrations took place throughout the country. In London a crowd of 15,000 marched to Wandsworth Prison. At the end of February, Shapurji Saklatvala, a Communist MP, presented Parliament with a petition for the prisoners' release signed by 300,000 people. And less than a month later, a meeting at the Albert Hall ('one of the biggest meetings ever held in London') rose to its feet and repeated after Lansbury the seditious slogans for which the Communists had been jailed;

> We call upon all soldiers, sailors and airmen to refuse under any circumstances to shoot down the workers of Britain, and we call upon working class men to refuse to join the capitalist army. We further call upon the police to refuse to use their batons on strikers or locked out workers during industrial disputes.[14]

On 12 February 1926, both the Miners' Federation and the Industrial Committee of the Trade Union Congress considered Walter Citrine's 'Memorandum on the Impending Crisis', which spoke of 'unmistakeable evidence of preparation for possible public disorder. The Fascisti movement is drilling and organising its forces'.[15]

It is in this atmosphere of potential civil strife, in which Bolsheviks are supposed to be squaring up to Fascists, and in which class warfare seems at long last about to burst openly upon the streets of Britain, that it becomes both proper and interesting to inspect the Shakespearean coordinates mentioned above. Within the Shake-speare Festival at Stratford there is a central highlight: the celebration on 23 April of the Bard's Birthday, marked by a civic luncheon, various public ceremonies, and the performance in the evening of a special Birthday Play at the Shakespeare Memorial Theatre. Less than two weeks after Citrine's alarming forecast of violent public disorder, there appeared in *The Times* of 25 February 1926 a simple but slightly disturbing announcement: 'For the Birthday Play . . . the Governors of the Theatre have chosen *Coriolanus*.'

Just over a week later, on 6 March 1926, and in mysterious circumstances, the Shakespeare Memorial Theatre at Stratford was burned to the ground.

Birthday Bard

By the end of the first quarter of the twentieth century, largely as a result of the sort of educational processes I have outlined above, Shakespeare had undoubtedly become established as a pillar of the existing social and political order in Britain; the linchpin of an education and examination system which, with the academic subject called 'English' at its centre, 'Englished' the world in a particular political mould. There is even a well-known comic verse which records a potent link between the study of Shakespeare, as determined by one of his most influential academic intermediaries, and the machinery of government accessible through the civil service examinations:

> I dreamt last night that Shakespeare's Ghost
> Sat for a civil service post.
> The English paper for that year
> Had several questions on King Lear,
> Which Shakespeare answered very badly
> Because he hadn't read his Bradley.

This appeared in *Punch* on 17 February 1926. Its author was Guy Boas (1896–1966), Vice President of the English Association and originator and Associate Editor (1935–65) of its journal *English*. Clearly, the flames which, less than three weeks later, consumed the Memorial Theatre in Stratford, also licked tentatively at a power–knowledge nexus lying at the heart of a national, not to say imperial culture.

Charged with the awesome duty of preserving and presenting work of such monumental design, the Shakespeare Company at Stratford showed commendable spirit. Undaunted by the fire, it took over a cinema, the Stratford Picture House, and continued its preparations for the season. Then, on 12 April, on the day the Festival opened, another bombshell exploded. The headlines of a local paper, the *Wolverhampton Express*, give the essence of it. 'Shakespeare Dragged into Politics' they cried. 'Inner Story of Strange Conflict'.

What the inner story revealed was that the Soviet Union had recently requested that it should be permitted to join that large group of nations whose flags are flown in the centre of Stratford in honour of Shakespeare, at the Birthday celebrations. Incensed at what she was to term a proposal for a 'profanation' of the town of the National Poet's birth, the wife of the Vicar of Stratford, a Mrs Melville, had organized a petition, collecting over 2,000 signatures, which demanded in vigorous terms that the Hammer and Sickle should not in any circumstances appear at the ceremony. The barrier between the Bard and Politics was suddenly breached, and the noise was deafening.

The redoubtable Mrs Melville pulled no punches. And in the course of her denunciation of the Soviet Union in the press, interesting aspects of her began to emerge. Not only was she vocal. Not only was she tough-minded. Not only was she (as the *Wolverhampton Express* felt compelled to inform its readers) 'Eton Cropped', and not only did she have strong objections to the socialist Bernard Shaw's frivolous suggestion that the burning down of the theatre was 'very cheerful news' (he offered to provide a list of other theatres which might, with profit, be similarly destroyed), she was also, she announced with pride, 'A Fascist and a Conservative'. And this said nothing of her role as chairperson of the local branch of the right-wing and notoriously anti-Semitic association known as the National Citizens' Union.[16]

'Will Soviet Red Flag be Unfurled?' 'Strong Attitude of Fascist Woman' screamed the *Wolverhampton Express*. Other papers, including *The Times*, were more temperate, but *The London Mercury*, edited by Sir John Squire, whose strong admiration for Fascism and whose 'overt championing of Mussolini' was well known, was highly approving.[17] But few of them stressed what is perhaps most interesting from our present point of view: Mrs Melville was also one of the governors of the Shakespeare Theatre, and thus presumably amongst those responsible for the choice of *Coriolanus* as the Birthday Play.

It is time to move to that occasion itself: 23 April 1926, and the performance of the Birthday Play, on the occasion of Shakespeare's Birthday, in Shakespeare's Birthplace. As we do so, perhaps it is worth pausing to ponder two of the fundamental implications of that time and that place.

First, Shakespeare's Birthday undoubtedly has a symbolic aura by reason of its date: 23 April. This is St George's Day, the patron saint of England. That national dimension of the Bard's beginning is reinforced by the standard biographical assertion that he obligingly died – no less symbolically – on the same day in 1616: 23 April. He is thus, by calendar, neatly consecrated top and tail, entrance and exit, to his native land in something of the same way that other great artists find themselves fused to their countries of origin. Louis Armstrong, for instance, always used to give as his birthday the entirely fictitious but no less significant date of 4 July 1900.

Second, the notion of birthplace, or seat of origin, as somehow a location of special sanctity and source, ultimately, of authority and authenticity, is a crucial matter. The example of Bethlehem is the most obvious of many. For if birthplaces can be said to fix, formulate and guarantee forever, they can stand as major fortifications against flux. They can be said to make us what we 'really' are, and to promise that nothing ever 'really' changes. Locating Shakespeare firmly and finally in Stratford is, like placing God in his heaven and the Queen on her throne, curiously comforting.

Against the willed permanence of these arrangements, the concrete change-making events of 23 April 1926 begin nevertheless remorselessly to lap. And the sound that insistently recurs is that of the crumbling of the barrier between Art and Politics. We can hear it most clearly if we interlace the events of the Birthday celebrations – as it were stereophonically – with those other incidents taking place in the world beyond Stratford, to which Stratford nevertheless felt itself to be speaking and of which it certainly thought itself to be representative. The major occurrences in that world were, of course, the political manoeuvrings that constituted the build-up to the by now inevitable General Strike. Sparked by the clash between coal-owners (their philanthropy for the moment distinctly in abeyance) and miners (fighting for a living wage), this finally began only ten days later, on 3 May. It lasted until 12 May. The General Strike was, it is worth recalling, the major public political demonstration of the century in Britain. Whatever the final outcome, at the time it provoked genuine fears of a Bolshevik revolution.

At 11 a.m. on 23 April, in London, Stanley Baldwin was presiding over a tense joint meeting of coal-owners and miners. In Stratford, at approximately the same time, the Birthday celebration ceremonies began. The flags of sixty-three nations (including that of the Soviet Union) were unfurled without incident. Indeed, a placatory wreath of violets, lilacs, roses and wistaria had already been received at Stratford from Soviet headquarters, and was placed on Shakespeare's tomb.[18]

There followed a public luncheon during the course of which the traditional toast to 'The Immortal Memory' of the Bard was proposed by Mr James Montgomery Beck, a former Attorney-General of the United States. Beck's right-wing politics were well known. An apostle of extreme individualism, he would later resign from one of Roosevelt's New Deal committees, aghast at what he saw as its radical tendencies. No doubt, when he told his fellow diners that 'a large body of Shakespeare's matchless verse reflected his own views on the moral problems of life', their digestive systems gurgled accord.[19]

That afternoon, in London, at 5.45 p.m., Baldwin and his Cabinet colleagues met a committee representing the coal-owners. Thomas Jones, Baldwin's Secretary, noted in his diary the 'contrast between the reception which Ministers give to a body of owners and a body of miners. Ministers are at ease at once with the former, they are friends jointly exploring a situation.' Somewhat taken aback, he asks whether it would be 'better to precipitate a strike or the unemployment which would result from continuing the present terms.'[20] At 7.15 p.m., Baldwin went to dinner – perhaps, on this evidence, having almost colluded in a decision to precipitate the strike. At roughly the same moment in Stratford, 'a company of mutinous Citizens, with staves, clubs, and other weapons' ran on to the stage of the Picture House. *Coriolanus* had begun.

Enter 'Shakespeare'

The *Morning Post* review of the next day (24 April) was characteristic of many responses in being oddly lame. Perhaps dissolution of the barrier between Art and Politics scarcely warrants the salute of a bang. What it certainly received was a cautious whimper: 'a play of arguments . . .' the reviewer pronounced, 'that in many ways seem strangely up to date'.

Coriolanus of course has its own 'political unconscious', and perhaps bears the marks of the social tensions surrounding its origins in 1607/8. In 1926, other pressures were certainly at work and the very choice of the play – perhaps the first move in an attempt, putting it baldly, to leap the Art–Politics divide and to hijack Shakespeare for a right-wing cause – could not help but make it seem 'strangely up to date'. But for it to function as the ideological weapon its promoters presumably wanted, then in the name of integrity and coherence specific aspects of its text would, in the event, have to be foregrounded at the expense of others.

For the text plunges us immediately into an arena where choices are urgently required: with concrete political confrontation occurring at street level, it has an urgency to match anything on offer outside the theatre. Uniquely amongst plays of the period, *Coriolanus* opens with a scene of public violence: the entry of that 'company of mutinous Citizens, with staves, clubs and other weapons'. This ever-present physical challenge to and questioning of the ties which bind a society together ironically undercuts all of its subsequent expositions of 'organic' theories of society, such as the fable of the belly presented by Menenius (I, i, 95ff.).

In short, there is no doubt that the play's central concern is the political one raised on the streets both in 1607 and in 1926: can mutually exclusive class interests ever be appeased? These political dimensions are reinforced by the central spectacle the play consistently presents of a figure who, contemptuous of society's demands, tries to 'opt out', to rise above it: one who himself undermines the co-operative imperatives of the fable of the belly by his habit of insulting his fellow organs and threatening to 'Hang 'em' (I, i, 180–204).

Caius Martius's concerted efforts to distinguish and separate himself from his society are marked not just by his use of such terms of strong rejection. The very feat on which his fame rests sees him entering the city of Corioles on his own, as a single morsel thrown in 'to the pot' (I, iv, 47) and being locked in there 'himself alone/To answer all the city' (ll. 50–1). And this singularity receives a confirming rhythmic stress throughout. His followers are urged 'alone' to follow him, to cry 'O me alone! Make you a sword of me!' (I, vi, 73–6). His reminder, 'Alone I fought in your Corioles walls' (I, viii, 8) is regularly taken up by others, 'alone he enter'd/The mortal gate of the city', 'aidless came off'(II, ii, 110–14) and on his return to Rome, that city is urged to 'Know Rome, that all alone Martius did fight' (II, i, 161). Faced with his greatest challenge, when his mother comes to plead with him finally to spare Rome, he reminds us in resonant terms of his continuing project: to stand at last absolutely alone, 'As if a man were author of himself/And knew no other kin' (V, iii, 36–7). The power of this validation of unique, personal identity, this sense of ultimately being true to an inner, self-authenticating subjectivity, finally enables Coriolanus to override the banishment to which Rome harshly subjects him. In the end, it fuels an astonishing conceptual reversal which completes the self-authoring, and decisively cuts him off from any contact with society:

> You common cry of curs! whose breath I hate
> As reek o' th' rotten fens, whose loves I prize
> As the dead carcasses of unburied men
> That do corrupt my air: I banish you!
> (III, iii, 120–3)

Absolute, even heroic, self-commitment in the face of a contemptible world in this manner, assertion of the individual solitary will as the ultimate and only valid instrument of power and morality, has of course been a feature of a range of political stances in Europe since the early modern period and is probably specifically linked with the thinking of Nietzsche. It readily produces the sort of creature described by J. P. Stern:

> The Will – not the common will of a body politic but *his* individual solitary will, mythologized to a heroic dimension – is his instrument. He is a maker of his kingdom: the powerful embattled personality . . . imposes its demands upon the world and attempts to fashion the world in its own image . . . His acts are judged according to a criterion of immanent, inward coherence: that is, according to the degree to which a man's utterances and actions express his total personality and indicate his capacity for experience.[21]

Stern is describing here not the character of Coriolanus, but the ideological seedbed from which sprang the phenomenon of Hitler. He proposes the German word *Erlebnis*, which refers to living experience, inner authentic conviction (*inneres Erlebnis*) to suggest the sense of that 'immanent inward coherence' on which such terrifying power rests. Coriolanus evidently possesses and glories in *Erlebnis* of this sort in ample measure. His celebration of it reaches its climax with his magnificent reminder to Aufidius of the distinctive basis of his fame. It lies precisely in what Hitler used to call *Front Erlebnis*, the personal, authentic, living experience of battle, crystallized in the moment when

> like an eagle in a dovecote, I
> Flutter'd your Volscians in Corioles.
> Alone I did it.
> (V, vi, 114–16)

'Alone I did it.' Words, no doubt, to gladden Mrs Melville's heart. Of course, the temptation to hear in this ultimate distillation of Coriolanus's megalomania the faintest striking of a political and psychological note whose furthest pitch sounds in the very title of Hitler's *Mein Kampf* should obviously be resisted. Nevertheless, as we have seen, the rise of Fascism in Germany during the period immediately preceding the General Strike in Britain certainly informed the political atmosphere in which that event took place. It even happens that the second and final volume of *Mein Kampf* was published in 1926.

Yet to present *Coriolanus*, chosen as the 1926 Birthday Play, as a validation, even a justification of this sort of lone, self-endorsing independence, to draw out the assertion of single subjectivity and unique heroic individualism in the face of the contemptible masses as its essence and its 'message' – as one kind of right-wing reading surely must – it is necessary at the same time to suppress other dimensions of the text. And, in fact, a contradictory case can easily be discerned, deployed no less forcefully in the play, which questions whether true independence is ever possible and suggests to the contrary that human beings are inescapably involved in mutuality and defined by reciprocity.

Coriolanus may, as his nomenclature allows, virtually become a city, but so after all do the plebeians. 'What is the city but the people?' says the Tribune Sicinius. 'The people are the city', they answer (III, i, 197–9). In effect, the apparent polarity 'Individual–Society' is constantly undercut (even deconstructed) in the play in a kind of counter-rhythm which syncopates with the assertions of 'alone'-ness and singularity. Gradually, the process expands to undermine a wide range of the oppositions on which Coriolanus's view of the world depends. Once Antium's enemy, he finds himself entering that city offering friendship, and saying 'O world, thy slippery turns . . . /My birthplace hate I, and my love's upon /This enemy town' (IV, iv, 13–24). In this text, 'slippery turns' predominate and finally characterize: everything seems capable of turning into its opposite. This is true both sexually (IV, v, 115–19) when Aufidius seems to love Coriolanus like a woman and when 'Our general himself makes a mistress of him' (IV, v, 199ff.: see also I, vi, 29–32) and socially when Coriolanus, perceived by servants as a beggar, turns into a hero in front of their eyes to the cry of 'Here's a strange alteration!' (IV, v, 149). By the end of the play, when we see the spectacle of 'patient fools,/Whose children he hath slain . . . giving him glory' (V, vi, 52–4) we realize that 'strange alteration' pinpoints the existential mode of someone who has finally been both a hero and a traitor on each side in the same war.

In short, Coriolanus can never finally be 'alone', or be the 'author of himself', because the very concepts at stake can only be generated in and be relevant to a society which must be presupposed. To mount the classic deconstructive argument, the opposition 'Individual–Society' has no validity. Only within the social structure, and conceived in its terms as its opposite, can 'alone' be meaningful. The very idea of individual subjectivity requires a society to validate it. And that requirement brings with it a commitment to language and thus to interlocution. To speak at all involves dialogue, the very condition of society. Nobody can speak meaningfully in a vacuum, because meanings are dialogically and socially – that is, politically – constructed. As a result, and as the play's 'slippery turns' and 'strange alterations' indicate, they are by no means fixed or permanent. What *Coriolanus* shows above all is that, lying at the heart of social structures and thus of politics, meaning is constantly in dispute, under discussion, and the battle for it is never-ending. Indeed, politics is to a large degree the name we give to that battle.

Of course, any 'reading' of a text can only be achieved by a suppression of the pluralities of which all texts are composed. That is how texts, and indeed languages, work. But there is a sense in which this latent plurality is exactly what *Coriolanus* finally makes overt. As a result, every attempt simply to shackle the play to a specific party-political position must run into crucial difficulties; something which Brecht discovered and which Günter Grass makes the subject of his own critique. Party-politics will always seek coherence. Yet few texts manage so blatantly as *Coriolanus* to promote those aspects of themselves that any coherent reading will try to suppress in order to establish its validity. The play doesn't simply focus on political struggle, it embodies political struggle. It isn't that it can be 'read' in a number of ways. It is that it can't be coherently read in any single way. And with this in mind, it's worth looking again at Caius Martius's magnificent assertion of his singularity, of his personal *Erlebnis*: his reminder that

> like an eagle in a dovecote, I
> Flutter'd your Volscians in Corioles.
> Alone I did it.
>
> (V, vi, 114–16)

Now, 'flutter'd' certainly seems to characterize the action of the heroic embattled individualist. An individual eagle pitted against a society of complacent doves, Coriolanus relentlessly harries them in the name of their enemy, just as he had proposed to do in the case of Rome. Yet the fact is that 'flutter'd' – to some degree the semantic fulcrum of this reading of the play – is a late emendation to the text which first appears in the Third Folio. The First Folio text of the play has 'flatter'd'.

However much ingenuity may be expended on justifying this emendation (almost universally adopted in modern editions), certain aspects of the situation are immediately clear. 'Flatter'd' makes perfect sense and needs no emendation if we accept the arguments made just now about Coriolanus's actual relation to his enemies and to society at large. The word suggests a much more complex interactive engagement with the Volscians than the imperiously dismissive 'flutter'd'. It implies comparison, evaluation and negotiation (the eagle's pre-emptive ferocity hinting at an unrealized potential in the doves) and thus a considerable degree of societal awareness and involvement. In short, it bespeaks a kind of baffled reciprocity and it acknowledges a degree of impotent mutuality, even whilst it manifests the wholesale hostility to which Coriolanus is undoubtedly committed. In this sense, 'flatter'd' is not simply different from 'flutter'd', it offers a completely opposed dimension of meaning. To refuse that dimension is deliberately to choose to impose a single and specific reading on the indeterminacy and multiplicity fostered by the First Folio text. The most obvious effect of replacing 'flatter'd' by 'flutter'd' is strongly to promote an uncomplicated sense of Coriolanus as unique individual pitted alone against society. Coriolanus the individualist, the single subject, the author of himself, would certainly 'flutter' the Volscians. But to 'flatter' them subtly undercuts and questions that role. In a play in which that kind of 'flattering' relationship is made an issue throughout, there is a sense in which the heart of the text lies here.

Some statistics may therefore be relevant. A glance at a *Concordance* reveals that the word 'flatter'd' (or 'flattered') appears fifteen times in Shakespeare's plays. Various forms of the verb 'to flatter' appear forty-seven times (seven of them in *Coriolanus*), together with a number of derivations such as 'flatterer', 'flatteries', 'flattery', etc. In *Coriolanus* the count for all the words in this category is as follows: 'flatter', 7; 'flatter'd' 1; 'flatterers', 2; 'flattery', 2. On the other hand, the word 'flutter'd' appears only once in the entire Shakespearean canon: here. There are no other occurrences of the word or its derivatives in any form, whether as noun, verb, adjective or anything else: no 'flutter', no 'flutter'd', no 'fluttering', no 'flutterers'.

What, then, are we to make of the decision of editors to replace 'flatter'd' by 'flutter'd'? The editor of the Arden edition of the play, for example, announces directly that the 'ambiguity' of 'flatter'd' strikes him as 'startling' and that he has changed it to 'flutter'd' in order 'to avoid eccentricity'.[22] This, of a play in which flattery, its complexities and its political and moral dimensions, is obviously a major consideration! Of course, any attempt to appropriate the text must appropriate this moment above all, and must do so by containing its ambiguity. Given this, the emendation of 'flatter'd' to 'flutter'd' perhaps begins to seem slightly less than innocent and even to hint at a tiny, occluded political dimension.

Conservative or right-wing readings of the play seem rooted in the nineteenth century where interpretations of it formed part of the 'struggle for possession of the national poet' mentioned by Jonathan

Bate. In the middle of that century, it was the actor Samuel Phelps who drained the lines of all duplicity and famously nailed the text down to a single meaning at this point by means of a reinforcing and deliberately delimiting gesture which Godfrey Turner describes as follows:

> A fine action of Phelps's accompanied his utterance of the word 'fluttered', which came after a seemingly enforced pause, and with that lifted emphasis and natural break in his voice, remembered, I dare say, by all who admired him in his prime. Lifting his arm to its full outstretched height above his head, he shook his hand to and fro, as in the act of startling a flock of doves.[23]

Let me be briefly outrageous. Let me suggest that Phelps's kinesic reinforcement of – indeed insistence upon – what for Shakespeare would at best be a nonce-word, 'flutter'd', represents a crucial moment of containment and enlistment. In it, the play is finally and irrevocably recruited to a conservative project in which the claims of single subjectivity are asserted against the collective demands of the state. It is not insignificant that Phelps's performance was first given in 1848, the year in which Charlotte Brontë wrote *Shirley* and, of course, the year of European revolutions. You might even say – as the faint echo of *Mein Kampf* drifts scandalously in and out of earshot – that the arm lifted in that vengeful salute has more than once found chilling echoes in the choreography of right-wing politics in our own century.

Yet, to retreat from the outrageous to its opposite in the English Midlands, how can we account for the apparent lameness of the response to the play's production in the charged atmosphere of Stratford in 1926? What is it that subverts – let us be bold – Mrs Melville's attempt to hijack it for the Fascist cause? Can it really be the case that, despite what we now know about events surrounding the Birthday celebrations, the machinations of Baldwin, the miners' leaders, the coal-owners, the theatre itself in flames, that the play's ultimate plurality finally drains away all its political force and leaves us just with – well, just with 'Shakespeare'?

For drain away it apparently did. On 7 May, two weeks after the Birthday Play had opened, and had entered the season's repertory, with the General Strike by now in full swing, angry crowds in the streets of large cities, volunteers driving buses and trains, food shortages, and provocative troop movements, the *Stratford-upon-Avon Herald* delivered itself of an editorial comment on the subject of the Shakespeare Festival and the Strike, in which its view of the barrier between Politics and Art, so precariously at stake in all the events of that Stratford spring, is nothing if not clear: 'It would be no bad thing', it fulminates, 'if the strikers themselves were brought in relays to see some of the Shakespearean productions.' The experience, it urges, 'might induce them to look beyond the paltry advantage of the moment and hitch their wagons to something more substantial than the will-o-the-wisp which is at the moment leading the country to irreparable ruin.'

You ain't heard nothing yet

No doubt the *Stratford-upon-Avon Herald* spoke for England. But perhaps it is mistaken to assume that its dismissal of the 'will-o-the wisp' of the General Strike and its recommended embrace of the 'more substantial' figure of Shakespeare constitutes, in the rather overheated atmosphere of the times, a bluff, good-hearted British rejection of Politics in favour of Art. Indeed, in its determined re-erection of the barrier dividing them, its own politics are perfectly clear. There are, after all, no such things as straightforward 'Shakespearean productions' in our society. Quite the reverse: a distinct political option exists which the invocation of 'Shakespeare' both commends and promotes. By and large it involves tradition, individualism, patriotism and permanence, all the ingredients of Mr Beck's Birthday luncheon speech dedicated to the 'Immortal Memory'. And it is far more powerful, seductive and acceptable than the politics any mere right-wing reading of *Coriolanus* could command. The medium, in this case, is certainly the message, and the essence of what might be called the 'Shakespeare Effect' lies in the more subtle, but also chilling principle that, whatever his plays say, 'Shakespearean productions' are always good for us. Their simple presence – like that of the Bard in Stratford – is enough.

Thus, the notion of *Coriolanus* as in itself a 'political' play is something of a nonsense. Of course, its overt 'subject' is politics. But a more genuinely disturbing prospect is the possibility that *all* Shakespeare's plays in our society have a political function, regardless of what their 'subjects' may be. In any case, we can never know what the exact response of the Stratford audiences to the production of *Coriolanus* in 1926 actually was. For instance, it could be said that, since *Coriolanus* is a play, it must in the end affirm the priority of society, in the very presupposition its nature makes manifest of a theatre in which and an audience before which it is performed. To the extent that it shows the assertion of individualism on the stage in front of an audience, it may enact the paradox which it explores, but it finally functions as an instrument of social cohesion.

But, and here a more complex dimension of the events of 1926 perhaps unexpectedly emerges, we should also remember that this particular Shakespearean production did not take place in a theatre at all. In fact, a deep-seated irony invests its actual venue and maybe the truly political dimension of the affair lies there. Hindsight – history's poor relation – tells us that the cinema is in many ways the theatre's opposite, and that it was also then to some extent its future. We might go even further and see in the advent of the cinema the perceptual and psychological outcrop of a material social revolution, unnoticed by Fascist and Bolshevik alike: the darkened auditorium and its lighted silver screen appropriate symbols for our modern society's growing paradoxical commitment to the sanctity of the inner – indeed the unconscious – life of the individual. It is not insignificant that by 1926 the expanding popularity of the medium meant that the Stratford Picture House offered the only hall large and central enough in the town for the production of *Coriolanus*.

A modern audience, committed to the cinematic mode, might well seek and find the fulcrum of that play in a moment which flatters (rather than flutters) its own preconceptions: the moment when, at the end of his mother's impassioned speech imploring him to desist from his intentions of sacking Rome, Coriolanus silently reaches for her hand, begins to weep, and then finally and famously capitulates to her wishes. In 1926, the Stratford Picture House was surely capable of lending those gestures a heightening cinematic quality. This is individualism in full cry, as it were, and the words 'O mother, mother!/What have you done?' (V, iii, 183–4) are surely the most suitable of all of Shakespeare's lines to appear as a caption on the silent screen, apparently offering insight into and validation of the purely individual dimensions of their utterer's agonized soul.

But if that remains a moment worthy only of D. W. Griffith, hindsight offers the further suggestion that the manipulative use of Art for political purposes was then only, in the massive terms in which we have since experienced it, in its infancy. The production of *Coriolanus* in Stratford, in 1926, in that cinema, designed though it undoubtedly was to link with the glorious past, was surely in effect also being propelled willy-nilly towards the inglorious future by a technological wind of change of which it knew little. But *we* know that within twelve months of that 1926 production, a series of frantic experiments that were taking place in Hollywood, California, finally bore fruit. And we can be fairly sure that the spectacle of another errant protagonist, kneeling at his mother's feet – indeed with an American version of 'O mother, mother!' on his lips – would shortly be able to yoke its audience, far more firmly than any Shakespearean productions could, to a set of comfortable stereotypes by which their political aspirations might be even more safely contained.

4   Take me to your Leda

Crash

Here are two voices: 'Give up literary criticism!' – the exasperation of a philosopher – and '*We* are not on trial; it is the system under which we live . . . It has broken down everywhere' – the desperation of a politician. Both utterances surfaced in the same year, and the peculiar resonance they retain for modern British and American ears probably results from the fact that the year was 1929. I open with them because the crisis of 1929/30 and its bitter fruit still finds sufficient parallels in our current situation to make any echoes from its depths somewhat disturbing. On that basis alone it would not be unreasonable to argue that the period marks a genuine watershed in the development of British ideology.

In May 1929 a general election had produced the second Labour Government (albeit a minority one). Confident, hopeful, even with Ramsay MacDonald at its head, it rode full tilt into the great Stock Market crash of October of that year, inheriting the débâcle that MacDonald's words attempt to grapple with: '*We* are not on trial; it is the system under which we live.' The apocalyptic atmosphere was heightened by the ungraspable nature of the breakdown. It was inexplicable, a text impossible to decipher. And when readings were forthcoming, the man and woman in the street found these difficult to understand and very far from reassuring. As the historian A. J. P. Taylor puts it, this was the year in which a perceptible 'cleavage' opened up between the assumptions of ordinary mortals on the one hand and academic and 'informed' opinion on the other which has lasted almost to the present.[1] Even the great revisionary economists, such as J. M. Keynes, had to accept a recondite specialism forced upon them by the crisis. 'Common sense' – the intellectual stock-in-trade of the ordinary mortal – seemed to have crashed along with the rest of the market.

For a potent emblem of the situation, one in which 'readings' and 'decipherments' are of the very essence, we need of course not so much to 'give up' literary criticism as to take up the nature of its manifestation in the academy, under the aegis of the subject called 'English'. For the period 1929/30 also saw the publication of two of the most influential academic works of our century: G. Wilson Knight's *The Wheel of Fire* and William Empson's *Seven Types of Ambiguity*.

Their fundamental premises could hardly have been more opposed, and if their publication in the same year helps to mark that 'common-sense' divide quite precisely for us, their discussion of a particular Shakespearean play indicates that, in effect, they stand on either side of it. Appropriately, the play is that study of system, trial and breakdown, *Measure for Measure*.

The appeal of Wilson Knight's 'Modernist' essay '*Measure for Measure* and the Gospels' in *The Wheel of Fire* can broadly be said to be to the 'ordinary mortal', and the play seems to offer no problems to this kind of common sense.[2] Seen as a wholly reassuring 'unambiguous' text, it apparently embodies a 'deliberate purpose'. That purpose involves the teaching of Christian morality, and Knight refers extensively to a fitting atmosphere 'pervading the play'. He sees the Duke as 'lit at moments with divine suggestion comparable with his almost divine power of foreknowledge and control and wisdom' and speaks of the 'ethical standards of the Gospels' being rooted in the play, with the 'evidently divine' Duke 'actually compared' to the 'Supreme power': his 'supernatural authority' making him 'exactly correspondent with Jesus' and 'automatically comparable with Divinity'.[3]

Seven Types of Ambiguity takes exactly the opposite view. Far from presenting the play as unambiguous, it cites a passage from *Measure for Measure* as an instance of ambiguity of the fifth type. This is the sort of ambiguity that denies any dimension of 'exact' correspondence to a text because it 'occurs when the author is discovering his idea in the act of writing'. The result is that the author is 'not holding it all in his mind at once, so that, for instance, there is a simile which applies to nothing exactly, but lies halfway between two things when the author is moving from one to the other.'[4]

The idea of a simile which applies 'to nothing exactly' but which lies 'halfway between two things' is challenging to say the least, and not the least of its challenges is to a common-sense notion of reading.

If Wilson Knight's is a 'Modernist' stance, Empson's could be called 'Post-modernist' by comparison. Certainly it raises fundamental questions about 'correspondence' and 'comparability'; about the way language works. Empson makes a point of refusing an obvious lifeline; the one which proposes a domesticated sort of ambiguity that shades into mere complexity, offering the reader two meanings for the price of one. In fact, he says quite categorically in a subsequent footnote that the fifth type of ambiguity 'does not assert that there would be alternative reactions to the passage when completely grasped, or that the effect necessarily marks a complex but integral state of mind in the author.' No; what it asserts is the absence of the integral and of the coherent: what it marks is the presence of what Empson directly terms 'confusion' and proceeds to describe as a serious and recurrent kind of 'logical disorder'. In short, this type of ambiguity results in nothing less than a complete breakdown of the common sense on which Wilson Knight's idea of 'exact correspondence' rests.

The passage in question involves those lines spoken by Claudio in Act I of the play in which, replying to Lucio, he admits that his own indictment and his imprisonment come directly

> From too much liberty, my Lucio, liberty;
> As surfeit is the father of much fast,
> So every scope by the immoderate use
> Turns to restraint. Our natures do pursue,
> Like rats that ravin down their proper bane,
> A thirsty evil; and when we drink we die.
>
> (I, ii, 117–22)

Empson's analysis of these lines pinpoints the issue:

> Evidently the first idea was that lust itself was the poison; but the word *proper*, introduced as meaning 'suitable for rats', but also having an irrelevant suggestion of 'right and natural'. . . produced the grander and less usual image, in which the eating of the poison corresponds to the Fall of Man, and it is drinking water, a healthful and natural human function, which it is intolerable to avoid, and which brings death. By reflection, then, *proper bane* becomes ambiguous, since it is now water as well as poison.[5]

Of course, the case can be pushed further: 'proper bane' is more than merely ambiguous. At stake is a wholesale contradiction between the concept of 'proper' or 'appropriate' and that of 'bane' in the sense of 'harmful', or fundamentally inappropriate. A genuine *aporia* looms in the text at this point. Applied to human beings, as it is by the simile, it represents a major challenge to integrity and coherence, well capable of bringing common sense crashing down. 'We are not on trial' – could it almost be the voice of Claudio we hear? 'it is the system under which we live'.

What emerges from this clash of readings of *Measure for Measure* might then form the basis for at least a minor revision of the history of literary criticism in our century. We in Britain are accustomed to hearing (and, some of us, to making) complaints concerning the depredations wrought by recent and fashionable French and American ideas upon the settled certainties of homespun critical analysis. Post-structuralism, Deconstruction, those great disintegrative movements from across the English Channel and the Atlantic Ocean, have suborned our youth – and our middle-aged – it is said, by pointing to the supposed chasms that underlie our logic, the contradictions that untune the strings of our meaning, the shifting intellectual sands on which the tents of our literary judgements are pitched. Yet, as we can see, if we read the evidence closely enough, the issues are much more deeply rooted in native soil, go back much further than a few years, and can be located in places much nearer home than Paris or New Haven. Here, in Britain, in that year of crisis, 1929/30, when things have 'broken down everywhere', certain familiar critical battle lines seem quite clearly drawn. And there is not a Frenchman in sight.

Goodnight, Vienna

Of course, *Measure for Measure* is a text that seems frequently to draw pointed commentary to itself. In fact, the persistence and sharpness of the disagreement over it might begin to suggest that the play periodically functions as a cultural arena in which significant ideological conflict takes place.

If that was true in 1929/30, another no less significant example erupted in the following decade, when L. C. Knights's essay, 'The ambiguity of *Measure for Measure*', appeared in *Scrutiny* in 1942.[6] Knights begins by voicing what by then had become a recurrent sense of disquiet: 'It is probably true to say that *Measure for Measure* is that play of Shakespeare's which has caused most readers the greatest sense of strain and mental discomfort'. This results, he claims, from an uneasy sense of paradox which prevails throughout; of conflicting 'truths' in the play whose antagonisms the text seems unable or unwilling to resolve.

The perplexity centres on the context of Claudio's supposed offence and, in particular, on the 'odd and inappropriate' way in which Claudio himself comments upon it. Knights finally focuses on exactly the lines that concerned Empson: Claudio's response to Lucio's enquiry about the cause of his imprisonment:

> From too much liberty, my Lucio, liberty;
> As surfeit is the father of much fast,
> So every scope by the immoderate use
> Turns to restraint. Our natures do pursue,
> Like rats that ravin down their proper bane,
> A thirsty evil; and when we drink we die.
>
> (I, ii, 117–22)

Drawn, like Empson, to that final simile, Knights concludes that it presents a crucial contradiction. Overtly, it proposes that, in respect of sexuality, human beings behave like rats. Made thirsty when they 'ravin down' poison, they continue to drink it, and so die. However, he goes on, since it is in our 'natures' to be prompted by sexual desire, the 'mere fact of being human' condemns us to 'ravin down', rat-like, that which dooms us. To be aware of this paradox, as human beings irrevocably are, is to confront insoluble dilemmas about the limitations that hedge social behaviour. For it finally raises general and disruptive questions about 'the relations of law and "justice", of individual freedom and social control, of governors and governed' (p. 229).

If the different readings of Wilson Knight and William Empson can be said to reflect some of the tensions of 1929/30, an initial response to L. C. Knights's reading would, of course, point out that the ambiguities and social paradoxes at which it worries are precisely those that, by 1942, the pressures of war were forcing to the centre of attention. Issues such as the bombing and general treatment of civilians, concentration camps, the requirements of military discipline, all combined to place the contradictions and uncertainties of the relation between individual freedom and social control at the head of any agenda, and it is perhaps unsurprising that such a text should be read in this way.[7]

In fact, it may even be somewhat surprising that a dissenting voice should be heard. Yet at the end of Knights's piece in *Scrutiny* we find – dread words – that the author has, he says, 'invited F. R. Leavis to develop his expressed dissent from the above. See the following page.' Turning to it, we find the well-known essay 'The greatness of *Measure for Measure*',[8] which Leavis subsequently reprinted in *The*

Common Pursuit (1952). Wholly rejecting all of Knights's reservations about the play, Leavis commits himself roundly to the view that it is simply 'one of the very greatest' of Shakespeare's works. He denies the existence of any damaging shortcomings, even to the extent of praising the play's dénouement as a 'consummately right and satisfying fulfilment of the essential design'.[9]

Knights, Leavis goes on, has unaccountably made 'heavy weather' of Claudio's lines about the reason for his imprisonment. He can see nothing 'odd' or 'inappropriate' in the simile of the 'rats that ravin down their proper bane', and reminds us that Claudio has committed what he calls a 'serious offence, not only in the eyes of the law, but in his own eyes'.[10] The play presents us, he concludes, with no contradiction, uncertainty or ambiguity. It does present us with complexity, which is a very different thing. But the central focus of that is not Claudio but Angelo.

In effect, Leavis's determination to scale contradiction and uncertainty down to the level of complexity – for that is what it amounts to – radically shifts the focus of the discussion and significantly re-contextualizes it. Knights's work, we should briefly recall, had come to prominence against a quite specific background: it had acted as the spearhead of the *Scrutiny*-based attack on an older, Oxford-dominated form of Shakespearean criticism represented by the writings of A. C. Bradley. Yet according to Leavis, Knights's essay now seems set to undermine the very principles in whose name that attack had been mounted. The charge must consequently be one of betrayal, or at least of culpable backsliding, for Knights's worried sense of the play's 'unsatisfactoriness' can only be explained, Leavis thunders, 'in terms of that incapacity for dealing with poetic drama, that innocence about the nature of convention and the conventional possibilities of Shakespearean dramatic method and form, which we associate classically with the name of Bradley'.[11] That this should come, as he points out, 'from the author of "How Many Children Had Lady Macbeth?" is the unkindest cut of all.

This 'literary critical' refocusing comes finally and fully to permeate and to determine Leavis's account of the play. Taking up what we might call the 'law and order' issue, for instance, he briskly dispatches its central features:

> We accept the law as a necessary datum, but that is not to say that we are required to accept it in any abeyance of our critical faculties. On the contrary it is an obvious challenge to judgement, and its necessity is a matter of the total challenge it subserves to

our deepest sense of responsibility and our most comprehensive and delicate powers of discrimination.[12]

The key operations recommended here – use of our 'critical faculties', exercise of 'judgement', 'responsibility' and of 'comprehensive and delicate powers of discrimination' – are of course exactly those which *Scrutiny* notoriously set out to promote as fundamental to the activity of literary criticism and the terms signal an immediately recognizable discourse in which they occupy a crucial position.

In short, we might say that Leavis's reading of *Measure for Measure* proves to be concerned less with the objective assessment of an 'essential' play than with a continuing debate about critical method originating from within the *Scrutiny* camp. L. C. Knights's account of the play makes an anguished Claudio the site of struggle and thus the centre of attention. It offers us an Angelo in whom an iron 'self-control' and a 'taut and strained' will prove the cause of Claudio's unhappy situation. It would be over-simple, I suppose, to suggest that, in his account of Angelo, Knights was already nervously sketching the Leavis he knew his essay would have to take on. And I shrink from the bald proposal that he saw himself as a compromised Claudio anxious, despite the evidence, to justify his crime. Perhaps more to the point is the fact that Leavis's account of the play makes Angelo the central figure. And his carefully reasoned sympathy for Angelo incorporates a recognition that the character offers a model with a broad moral application beyond the play. With his comment 'If we don't see ourselves in Angelo, we have taken the play and the moral very imperfectly',[13] sympathy intensifies into an odd kind of identification. Leavis's self-appointed role in *Scrutiny* as Shakespeare's lieutenant, charged with the strict enforcement of the Bard's meaning in his absence, perhaps reinforces that impression. And it may finally be not entirely mischievous to suggest that within the compass of Leavis's Angelo-like perception of the backsliding Claudio who 'has committed a serious offence' for which harsh punishment is due, we might just glimpse the recalcitrant figure of Knights.

At this point, then, the play's location threatens to become wholly Englished: Vienna, we might almost say, seems about to turn into Cambridge.

Legal fiction

In one sense, of course, it already had. One of the signal events of the crucial year of 1929/30 had been the re-establishment in Cambridge of the Viennese philosopher Ludwig Wittgenstein. Wittgenstein's return to Cambridge not only marked a significant development in the impact of a particular sort of philosophy, it also signalled a new level of engagement in a battle as old as Plato: that between the rival claims to knowledge advanced by the poet on the one hand and by the philosopher on the other.

In the Cambridge of 1929 the issues were sharply focused. If the sort of philosophy represented by Wittgenstein had in a sense emerged victorious from the defeat of idealism in the early years of the century, the study of 'creative', 'poetic' writing – literature – institutionalized in the new academic subject called English, was also the product of a conflict, but a much bloodier one. In the words of F. L. Lucas,

> It was . . . in March 1917, while the German armies were falling back to the Hindenberg Line, while Russia was tottering into Revolution and America preparing for war, that at Cambridge members of the Senate met to debate the formation of an English Tripos[14]

Certainly, the shape taken by the subject at Cambridge was decisively influenced by that conflict, to the extent that philological engagement with the language (a staple of the Oxford and London courses) was rejected as an unwholesome Teutonic pursuit.

F. R. Leavis must unquestionably rank as one of the most forceful proponents of that new School's principles, and his repeated claims on its behalf to a superior kind of knowledge always stressed a principled opposition to the rival claims of philosophy. Few more succinct examples of it are available than his flat declaration: 'philosophers are always weak on language'. Against this may be set what he calls his 'opposing conviction . . . that the fullest use of language is to be found in creative literature, and that a great creative work is a work of original exploratory thought'.

These of course are lifelong views, but I have taken the particular expression of them here from an essay written late in Leavis's career. In fact, the essay is devoted to his memories of Wittgenstein.[15] It consists largely of anecdotes and reflections, with a number of them quite firmly located in 1929. One of the most fascinating stories actually records an encounter between the German-speaking philosopher and the new discipline of English literary criticism. Curiously enough, the subject of the discussion was a poem by William Empson. Leavis takes up the story:

> He said to me once (it must have been soon after his return to Cambridge): 'Do you know a man called Empson?' I replied: 'No,

but I've just come on him in *Cambridge Poetry 1929*, which I've reviewed for *The Cambridge Review*.' 'Is he any good?' 'It's surprising', I said, 'but there are six poems of his in the book, and they are all poems and very distinctive.' 'What are they like?' asked Wittgenstein. I replied that there was little point in my describing them, since he didn't know enough about English poetry. 'If you like them,' he said, 'you can describe them.' So I started: 'You know Donne?' No, he didn't know Donne. I had been going to say that Empson, I had heard, had come up from Winchester with an award in mathematics and for his Second Part had gone over to English and . . . had read closely Donne's *Songs and Sonnets*, which was a set text. Baulked, I made a few lame observations about the nature of the conceit, and gave up. 'I should like to see his poems', said Wittgenstein. 'You can,' I answered; 'I'll bring you the book.' 'I'll come round to yours,' he said. He did soon after, and went to the point at once: 'Where's that anthology? Read me his best poem.' The book was handy; opening it, I said, with 'Legal Fictions' [*sic*] before my eyes: 'I don't know whether this is his best poem, but it will do.' When I had read it, Wittgenstein said, 'Explain it!' So I began to do so, taking the first line first. 'Oh! I understand that' he interrupted and, looking over my arm at the text, 'But what does this mean?' He pointed two or three lines on. At the third or fourth interruption of the same kind I shut the book, and said, 'I'm not playing.' 'It's perfectly plain that you don't understand the poem in the least,' he said. 'Give me the book.' I complied, and sure enough, without any difficulty, he went through the poem, explaining the analogical structure that I should have explained myself, if he had allowed me.[16]

Certain aspects of this narrative surely demand our attention. The literary critic's nervous policing of the boundaries of his own newly-established discipline is of course immediately apparent. A mystifying smoke-screen at once comes down. The philosopher's initial reconnaissance, which seeks intelligence of Empson's poems, draws withering tracer fire: 'they are all poems and very distinctive'. A patrol probing the nature of this distinction runs into the bayonets of a thin red line: 'I replied that there was little point in my describing them, since he didn't know enough about English poetry.' To the flanking movement of 'If you like them . . . you can describe them', the response is the heavy artillery of condescension: the philosopher would first need to know about Donne, and then about the English syllabus, if not about England (the casual mention of a famous and exclusive English public school threatens escalation of the conflict almost to the level of germ warfare). What possible sanctions can make an impression on the impenetrably foreign? A slightly languid note of *noblesse oblige* tempers the final bugle call: 'I made a few lame observations about the nature of the conceit, and gave up.'

Empson's poem nevertheless proves highly significant in respect of the symbolic dimensions of that skirmish. For 'Legal Fiction' turns out to be a work to which the issues of textual interpretation and of critical reading are themselves central. Its main concern, as its title suggests, is the Law, and the processes by which legal texts seem to construct narrative – and fictional – accounts of the status on earth of the human animal:

> Law makes long spokes of the short stakes of men.
> Your well fenced out real estate of mind
> No high flat of the nomad citizen
> Looks over, or train leaves behind.

Despite the consoling stories told by the law and its texts, the poem seems to say, human beings have no essential, transcendent rights that can be permanently guaranteed on earth. Our stakes in the world are temporary and short, regardless of what lengthy legal pronouncements ('long spokes') may suggest. Irrevocably implicated in the earth's unfathomable destiny, we are in no position to form any clear 'well fenced out' objective assessment of its nature, or to make substantial claims upon it. The *real* 'estate' which humanity genuinely inherits involves dizzying, incomprehensible reaches, well beyond the scope of the law's puny narratives:

> Your rights extend under and above your claim
> Without bound; you own land in Heaven and Hell;
> Your part of earth's surface and mass the same,
> Of all cosmos' volume, and all stars as well.

> Your rights reach down where all owners meet, in Hell's
> Pointed exclusive conclave, at earth's centre
> (Your spun farm's root still on that axis dwells);
> And up, through galaxies, a growing sector.

In fact, the earth has no permanent continuing centre despite the concentric, globe-like, firmly patterned structure (hinted at in that image of 'long spokes') that legal 'fiction' constructs. And beyond that, there lies no 'real' final presence or essential central core of individual subjectivity to substantiate the law's claims. In fact,

You are nomad yet; the lighthouse beam you own
Flashes, like Lucifer, through the firmament.
Earth's axis varies; your dark central cone
Wavers, a candle's shadow, at the end.

Wittgenstein's shamingly effortless exposition of Empson's dis-turbing, deconstructive thesis – achieved without benefit of 'English' or of Englishness – clearly carried a threat to which Leavis's efforts at closure and composure represent an uneasy response. That Wittgen-stein is here mocking, as philosopher, the practice of one kind of literary criticism emerges clearly enough in his repeated needling of Leavis in the name of just the sort of essentialist reassurances that the poem 'Legal Fiction' itself denies: 'Explain it! . . . Oh! I understand that. . . . But what does this mean?' Leavis's ill-tempered opting-out, 'I'm not playing', paradoxically gives the game away, and can stand as that sort of criticism's evidently ineffectual response to philo-sophy's upsetting investment in the notion of language 'games'. Against Leavis's dismissive 'philosophers are always weak on lan-guage', we must therefore set Wittgenstein's shattering, resonant retort; 'It's perfectly plain that you don't understand the poem in the least . . . Give me the book.'

Throwing off, at this moment, an apparently playful disguise, the returning philosopher suddenly emerges as an authoritative and sternly compelling figure, fully able to command the intricacies of texts about the law, and indeed perfectly capable of demonstrating this to an astonished upstart who, in his absence from the city, has temporarily usurped his powers. If Cambridge *were* Vienna, no Angelo could have been more disconcerted.

Putting on some English

It is hardly necessary to point out that Empson's poem effectively confronts the philosopher and the critic here with issues that are central to *Measure for Measure* itself. Both texts deal with the matter of 'legal fiction' in that both rehearse the notion of 'laws' whose unity and coherence proves not permanent, immutable or God-given, so much as the result of particular and contingent practices of reading.

In the case of Empson, the point is made that the 'real' estate of human beings may be read spiritually ('you own land in Heaven and Hell') as well as materially to a degree that mocks legal pretensions to deal solely in terms of attested, substantial 'fact'. In *Measure for Measure*, in the case both of Claudio and Angelo, a differently conceived reading of the law enshrined in the concept of the *sponsalia per verba de praesenti* in the one case or *de futuro* in the other, challenges and problematizes throughout the play the kind of legality on which Angelo bases his reign of terror.[17]

By insisting on the 'letter' of the law in the face of an opposing, older, common-law tradition of oral 'handfast' commitment which could be said to reflect its 'spirit', Angelo commits himself to a reading of the legal text which constructs it as unified, coherent, objective and distinctive: 'It is the law, not I, condemn your brother' (II, ii, 80). But of course, such a reading of the law can hardly be separated from the 'I' who undertakes it. Indeed, it surreptitiously generates and validates a particular version of that 'I', construed as an individual subject, at the mercy of specific fleshly promptings: appetites which, having determined, the law then proceeds to condemn. As Claudio rightly complains, laws read thus inevitably generate the crimes they punish, producing the paradox of the 'proper bane': that double-bind in which what must be avoided proves to be coterminous with what is unavoidable.

Wittgenstein's remarkable performance as an analyst of the 'analogical structure' of Empson's poem might be said to hint, despite Leavis's coolness, at a capacity for higher things. And indeed, without even applying for the necessary visa from Downing College, the philosopher did later proceed to a series of spirited engagements with Shakespeare. In them, the same kind of 'analogical' structures continued to attract his interest. In fact, with an unnerving directness quite alien to the felicitous Arnoldian mode favoured by most true-born English critics, he goes straight, as it were, for the poetic jugular:

> Shakespeare's similes are, *in the ordinary sense*, bad. So if they are all the same good – and I don't know whether they are or not – they must be a law to themselves.[18]

By this, Wittgenstein seems to mean that both the equivalences proposed by Shakespeare's poetic devices and those analogically put forward by the plays at large (to push his word *Gleichnisse* to its broadest reach) fail to match reality with much precision. That they therefore rank as 'bad' (he uses the uncompromising German word *schlecht*) strikes him as an obvious conclusion, whose only surprising feature is that it doesn't appear to be have been reached by everybody. In fact, as he points out, 'a thousand professors of literature' unaccountably share an opposite conviction. This prompts the suggestion that perhaps in Shakespeare's case, his adequacy in respect of reality, that vaunted 'truth to life' in which we can 'see ourselves', and perhaps even go on to make the peculiar sort of sympathetic identification experienced by Leavis in the case of Angelo, simply isn't relevant: 'you just have to accept him as he is if you are going to be able to admire him properly, in the way you accept nature, a piece of scenery for example, just as it is.'[19]

We should, Wittgenstein seems to be proposing, cease to regard Shakespeare as – that legal fiction – a coherent, individual personality intent on the exact sympathetic recording of an essential and experienced 'real' world. We would do better to start thinking of him more as an inanimate, inexplicable feature of our cosmos, like a mountain, or a piece of scenery, something which is first and foremost simply *there*. The evident 'badness' of Shakespeare's similes (and to his credit, Wittgenstein never abandons that judgement) then poses no problem. They are, as he puts it, a law to themselves. And we can content ourselves with staring 'in wonder'[20] at a Bard whose standing is that of a 'spectacular natural phenomenon' rather than a 'human being'.[21]

It is important, of course, to place Wittgenstein's remarks in context, and when we do so, this wholly alien view of Shakespeare takes on a special significance. Most of the comments I've quoted come from notes made during or just after the Second World War. As a Jew, as a former citizen of Vienna, and as a native speaker of German, Wittgenstein would have had a sense of the full horror of those years and the incapacity of language to prove 'exactly correspondent' to it that few of his Cambridge colleagues could have appreciated.

Wittgenstein's personal alienation was by this time virtually total. The issue of his own sexuality may or may not have been a cause of some difficulty, but of course he was fully estranged from the fundamental precepts of his earlier philosophy. This rather daunting reality is surely part of a range of experience that he finds Shakespeare's plays inadequate to match, and his irritation at the 'thousand professors of literature' who thought otherwise is at least understandable.

One of them, like it or not, must have been F. R. Leavis. For by 1942, as we have seen, a newly professionalized academic literary criticism had been firmly established in Britain under the aegis of the subject called 'English'. In fact, Leavis must have been one of the first teachers at Cambridge actually to have taken a degree in that subject and then to have taught it for a living. Perhaps it is not unreasonable, looking back at his account of *Measure for Measure*, to suggest that it is finally and conclusively determined by a context which, wholly excluding Wittgenstein and his alien philosophical concerns, can be said, in both a literal and a metaphorical way, to put 'English' on the play.

I intend here both the American colloquial sense of 'English' as a bias applied, say, to a ball, to cause its path to swerve, and also a British sense of the word which – in a tradition extending from Arnold through Eliot to its climax (and perhaps its conclusion) in Leavis – perceives 'English' as an academic subject wholly unlike any other, in that it can be held to function as the sacred repository of the traditions and values of an entire national culture. In its British context, of course, putting on 'English' in this way not only excludes a Teutonic Wittgenstein and satisfactorily confirms an irredeemable 'weakness' in respect of language. It also excludes, in a process of systematic, even purposive alienation, numerous native-born British people (Welsh, Scottish, Irish) – to say nothing of those whose inherited Englishness regrettably falls beyond the Cambridge pale. But perhaps the time seemed ripe. In 1942, the year of Leavis's *Scrutiny* piece on *Measure for Measure*, English was less than twenty-five years old at Cambridge but *Scrutiny* was exactly ten. In the very next issue of the journal, that anniversary was celebrated with an Angelo-like commitment to the rigorous and combative prosecution of the battle for an English 'ideal of civilization'.[22]

However, implacable adversaries lay in wait. In December 1942 the Beveridge Report appeared, with its commitment to a new vision of social democracy and the welfare state. In the same year, R. A. Butler was appointed to the Ministry of Education and began the work which was to lead to the famous Butler Education Act of two years later. By opening up the grammar schools and ultimately the universities to large sections of the population hitherto denied those benefits (a development which the novelist Evelyn Waugh later characterized as the awarding of 'degrees to the deserving poor') this would prove a major instrument in the ultimate betrayal, in Leavis's terms, of the embattled English culture whose defender *Scrutiny* had claimed to be. Indeed, in the subsequent years in *Scrutiny*'s pages, we can follow Denys Thompson as he gloomily rummages for metaphors that might correspond to a sense of national collapse treacherously engineered by alien forces. If the harsh yoke of equal opportunity was going to be imposed on the island race by a vengeful enemy from within (the Labour Government no less) then – Thompson finally lights upon the *mot juste* – a whole set of ancient moral and political principles would find themselves 'pearlharboured' as a result.[23]

Swan-song

As a child of the Butler Education Act, this essay and this book ample evidence of the appalling catastrophe it generated, perhaps I may be permitted to smile – even inscrutably – at that. Let me go on to suggest, from the vantage point of fifty years on, that Leavis's 'Englished' account of *Measure for Measure* has possibly found itself overtaken by a peculiarly English fate; has been 'dunkirked', it might be said, by elements also from within, with Cambridge playing its by now traditional subversive role. I am speaking not of the shades of Burgess and Maclean, Philby and Blunt – all of whom passed through the university in these years – but of the implications of the work of that no less subversive Cambridge pair, Empson and Wittgenstein.

Wittgenstein's interest in Empson was reciprocated. In fact, Empson once slyly arranged for Wittgenstein to make a curious personal appearance in a poem of his called 'This last pain':

> 'What is conceivable can happen too',
> Said Wittgenstein, who had not dreamt of you . . .

If we wanted to pin down the sort of game Wittgenstein was playing with Leavis, this perhaps offers a clue. Truth, these lines seem to imply, is a matter of projection as much as perception. It is conceived, not found: made by the mind, not discovered by it. A world of objective, unprocessed, uninterpreted 'reality' is not and never has been available to us. Whatever is conceivable can happen because the conceivable constitutes the condition and the limit of our perception and awareness. It is a principle as old as Vico, to which the term *verum factum* applies: that which we regard as true is that which we have ourselves made. In this poem, Empson appears not only to accept that state of affairs. He even counsels that we should, whatever disappointment may be involved, nevertheless make it the basis of a life-style: we should, as he puts it in the same poem, 'learn a style from a despair'.

For Wittgenstein, the doctrine of *verum factum* had its implications for literary language, as it did for life-style, and we might suspect that these lurk, again memorialized for us in Leavis's account, within a classic peremptory injunction with which on one occasion he confronted the dumbfounded critic. It is the challenge with which we began: 'once,' says Leavis, 'he came to me and, without any prelude, said "Give up literary criticism!" [24]

Leavis's uncharacteristic response – silence – is garnished in the telling with a good deal of defensive *esprit de l'escalier* whose purpose seems once more to be the policing of boundaries: 'I abstained from retorting, "Give up philosophy, Wittgenstein!" largely because that would have meant telling him that he had been listening to the talk of a dominant coterie, and ought to be ashamed of supposing that Keynes, his friends and their *protégés* were the cultural élite they took themselves to be.' But even as it turns in disgust from the academic, specialized and non-commonsensical world of such as Keynes, that response sadly misses the point.

The point is surely that to Wittgenstein the sort of literary criticism which Leavis was coming to represent at that time seemed an obvious blind alley. It might as well be given up, for what Wittgenstein means by literary criticism here is the sort of thing he can already do perfectly well – to Leavis's surprise, when he 'explains' the 'analogical structure' of Empson's poem.

Wittgenstein's value to us as native speakers of English lies precisely in the fact that his vision is a distinctive, un-English, un-British, un-American and alien one. He subscribes, as we have seen, to none of those assumptions about Shakespeare's essential 'greatness' or 'truth to life' that constitute the inheritance of the English or the preference of the Anglophile. His encounters with the Bard are profitably 'outlandish': they take place beyond the barbed wire of that 'English' front line behind which most of us crouch. And his comments make manifest a position with whose implications we are only relatively recently – in Britain – coming to terms. That is, that to the uninvolved, alienated eye, no text offers values or meanings that exist as essential features of itself. Shakespeare's plays are not essentially this or essentially that, or essentially anything. They are, to take up Wittgenstein's metaphor, far more like natural phenomena, mountain ranges, pieces of scenery, out of which we *make* truth, value, 'greatness', this or that, in accordance with our various purposes. Like the words of which they are composed, the plays have no essential meanings. It is *we* who mean, *by* them.

If Wittgenstein's thinking thus urges us to 'give up' the idea that language 'represents' an essential reality to which 'explanation' can open the door, it demands by implication that we cease to 'divinize' the universe, as Richard Rorty has put it, by the presupposition of an ultimate, divinely authenticated reality that can finally be thus revealed.[25] In respect of literary texts made out of language, one sort of criticism can be said to have long since arrogated to itself a similar 'divinizing' function, its central presupposition a God-like author whose hidden meaning remains to be revealed or 'explained' by a priestly critic.

The notion of Shakespeare as a sort of disguised Duke-like deity, inseminating his Viennese subjects with eternal truths brought ultimately to birth by the midwifely ministrations of an Angelo-style literary critic, is not of course an uncommon one, and part of my point is that it lurks undetected as an animating force in a good many twentieth-century accounts of Shakespeare – in particular those of Wilson Knight and F. R. Leavis to which I've been referring.

Knowing analysts will already have detected an oddly mixed metaphor here, deriving partly from *Measure for Measure*, but mostly from the ancient figure of Zeus who, disguising himself as a swan, rapes the beauteous Leda. She, Yeats tells us, lacking the services of a literary critic, remained unfortunately ignorant of the true import both of the impregnating act and of its outcome.

But perhaps we should be less condescending, less dismissive than Yeats of Leda's potential as a positive, not to say resistant element in an arrangement whose fundamental opposition cries out in any case to be unpicked. The over-simple disposition of active and passive roles presupposed by it should at least alert us to the possibility that its main function is to generate and sustain the demeaning relationship which it purports only to describe. For the truth is that such an opposition – which makes no allowance for Leda's non-compliance or principled oppugnancy – is, like most others, not immutable, absolute or permanent, and we have *Measure for Measure* to remind us of that: a play whose very title hints at the potential for swivelling or turning contained in every conceptual polarity, and whose narrative gives ample evidence of its always possible occurrence. As every liberty slithers towards imprisonment, as every 'scope' turns into restraint, Claudio's account of the condition he terms our 'proper bane' must bring to mind the permanency of the impermanence that involves us all: of that perpetual swivelling motion in which opposites are continuously open to be depolarized, realigned, with the sense they purport to weave accordingly unravelled to a degree that makes the straightforward communication of pre-packaged, coherent and unified 'meaning' seem an impossible project.

To abandon the project is of course to reject the notion of an essential, given, even God-given 'meaning' for any play, and to bring seriously into question the model of a coherence-generating one-way transaction in which the writer's work supposedly deals, and in whose name his Zeus-like (and inevitably male) fertilization of the Leda-reader takes place. As Empson shows when, at his most deconstructive, he is prepared to read a Shakespearean simile as fundamentally incoherent, and as Wittgenstein demonstrates when, similarly disposed, he is prepared to read Shakespeare's similes as 'bad', those roles need at least to be problematized. They might even be reversed. In short, the reader can, should, and, some might say, always does resist the writer, reject his avian advance, throw off his feathered embrace, and take the initiative in making the text mean.

Does this suggest that in 1929/30, that year of crisis, we find ourselves confronted by the end of one notion of the literary process, its swan-song, perhaps, in the mellifluous Modernist pages of *The Wheel of Fire*? And at the same time, do the spiky, uncomfortable sentences of *Seven Types of Ambiguity* ring in the new – the Post-modern song of Leda in which no Zeus is good Zeus?

Of course, 1929/30 is an obvious candidate for the Year of The Reader in any case. It saw, after all, the publication of another major work of literary criticism, one in which, for the first time in the Anglo-American tradition, the reader achieved pride of place: I. A. Richards's *Practical Criticism*. Nevertheless, more than sixty years on, the central issues remain unresolved, at least in the English-speaking world. Where does the initiative finally lie? With the writer or with the reader? And whose side are we ultimately on: that of Zeus and the Swan, or that of mere mortals and of Leda? Could we, as inveterate sifters of texts, ever respond to the full urgency of Wittgenstein's counsel? If we give up one sort of literary criticism, will it not always be necessary to swivel to an alternative? Indeed, is not to 'give up literary criticism' to take up a specific critical position? Should it turn out to be the case that 'the system under which we live . . . has broken down everywhere', one thing alone is certain: if we wish Leda to become our leader we can hardly also hope to remain, as the French might say, *du côté de chez Swan*.

5   Slow, slow, quick quick, slow

Whispering grass

Mr Walsh scratched his rather prominent nose. He could hardly believe his luck. The life of an officer in the British Secret Service, he perhaps reflected, was not over-endowed with opportunities for decisive intervention in international affairs. But now, acting on information received, the Home Secretary's office had dispatched him to investigate a group of persons who had recently rented a house near a vulnerable part of the British coastline. Their behaviour was suspicious. They might well be spies. And an arrest seemed likely.

The information had initially come from a Dr Lysons of Bath in letters dated 8 August and 11 August, which referred to the activities of what appeared to be an 'emigrant family'. A dark-skinned man and a 'woman who passes for his sister' had been heard speaking in strange accents and seen roaming the cliffs with camp stools and 'a Portfolio'. On 11 August, in his report to Mr King, Permanent Under-Secretary for the Home Department, Mr Walsh outlined his conclusions that the suspects were indeed foreigners, 'French people' no less.

However, further investigation revealed to Mr Walsh, as he reports on 15 August, that this was 'no French affair'. What confronted him, and what had affronted the locals, was nothing less than 'a mischievous gang of disaffected Englishmen'. He adds that he has established the identity of the person who had rented the house, as well as the make-up of a group of potential subversives and terrorists who were living nearby and who frequently visited it. The former's name was Wordsworth. The latter consisted of a 'sett of violent Democrats' and included a 'Mr. Coldridge'. To compound the apparent felony, and as a sure indication of guilt, this creature, 'recounted a Man of superior Ability', was known to be 'frequently publishing'.[1]

The year was 1797. Rumours of a French invasion were rife. Coleridge and his family were living close to the Bristol Channel at Nether Stowey in Somerset, the Wordsworths had taken a house at Alfoxton nearby, and the locals had recognized amongst the visitors to this band of alien intellectuals the notorious radical John Thelwall, who had recently been tried for high treason.

A powerful irony invests the fact that the information laid against Coleridge and Wordsworth was provided by precisely the sort of people they were writing about, indeed admiring for the un-corrupted nature of their language, in *The Lyrical Ballads*. While the poets wandered the grassy hills of Somerset, the locals – noting, as the reports indicate, their 'want of ocupation', their love of country walks, their notebooks, their campstools, their sketches, their inquisi-tiveness – concluded that they were foreigners. Inspired by fears of an invasion from France, to say nothing of a spontaneous overflow of powerful feelings, they proceeded to conduct an extraordinary whispering campaign against them which culminated, amongst those grassy banks, in 'grassing' of a quite different – if no less genuinely rustic – kind. Rarely has the idea of the poet or intellectual as alienated, detached, even 'foreign' observer taken so absurd a form as in the ludicrous case of these Cambridge 'spies' *avant la lettre*. Beyond it lies a serious issue: the manner in which the various discourses whose confrontations constitute the ideological battle-grounds of a culture reconnoitre, patrol, and construct intelligence reports of each other's front-line manoeuvres. Clearly, some aspects of the discourse of 'ordinary men' were misread by the poets. Clearly, the compliment was returned. Years later, Coleridge's uneasily Shakespeareanized account of the affair attempts to focus lightheartedly on Mr Walsh's activities in just these terms:

> The dark guesses of some zealous *quidnunc* met with so con-genial a soil in the grave alarm of a titled Dogberry of our neighbourhood, that a spy was actually sent down from the Government *pour surveillance* of myself and friend . . . He had repeatedly hid himself, he said, for hours together behind a bank at the seaside (our favourite seat) and overheard our conversation. At first he fancied that we were aware of our danger; for he often heard me talk of one *Spy Nozy* which he was inclined to interpret of himself, and of a remarkable feature belonging to him; but he was speedily convinced that it was the name of a man who had made a book and lived long ago.[2]

But whilst the discourse of political surveillance only looks foolish when it turns the philosopher Spinoza into a long-nosed undercover agent of a foreign power, Coleridge's account of the magistrate's examination of the landlord of the village inn has a more directly disturbing ring and suggests a metaphor and a role:

> Answer the question, sir! Does he ever harangue the people? . . . Has he not been seen wandering on the hills towards the Channel, and along the shore, with books and papers in his hand, taking charts and maps of the country? . . . Speak out man! don't be afraid, you are doing your duty to your King and Government. What have you heard? *Landlord:* Why, folks do say, your honour, as how that he is a *Poet.*[3]

Sweethearts on Parade

The image of the poet as 'spy', the sense of a connection between 'creative' writing and reading and covert analysis and 'policing', runs unannounced through a good deal of modern British verse, occasionally half-surfacing in texts such as the above, or in Browning's 'How it Strikes a Contemporary':

> The town's true master if the town but knew!
> We merely kept a Governor for form
> While this man walked about and took account
> Of all thought, said and acted, then went home
> And wrote it fully to our Lord the King

Spies, poets and critics have a good deal in common after all. To some extent, the activity of espionage has always involved the detailed sifting and critical 'decoding' of texts, the teasing out of ambiguities, the probing of the sort of occluded 'meanings' that emerge when the underpinnings of a discourse come into view. It is barely surprising to learn that the highly influential Department of English at Yale University acted as the seed-bed for the production of United States intelligence agents during and after the Second World War.[4]

Yet even between – most seriously between – speakers of the same language, the process has its hazards. The English language has always offered rich opportunities for American and British pronunciation or usage to generate discursive mismatchings the equal of those experienced by Wordsworth and Coleridge, and the banalities marking cultural difference on that linguistic level have long since found their way into popular song:

> You say Tomayto and I say Tomahto
> You say Potayto and I say Potahto
> Potayto, Potahto, Tomayto, Tomahto
> Let's call the whole thing off

But, as the case of Spy Nozy suggests, so-called serious writers of literature have never been immune from such depredations. This is Julian Maclaren-Ross's account of a conversation between himself and Graham Greene concerning the latter's film criticism; in particular, an article which centred on the film *Marked Woman*, featuring Eduardo Ciannelli, Humphrey Bogart and Bette Davis:

> I said: 'You based your article on the resemblance between the city under gangster rule and the feudal system, Ciannelli being the latterday equivalent of the Robber Baron.'
>
> 'I believe I did. Bogart as the crusading DA made the comparison actually, it was in the dialogue.'
>
> 'But you see', I said, 'it wasn't.'
>
> We had finished the coffee and brandy and were now drinking up the remainder of the beer. It was, perhaps, not an awfully wise mixture and may have gone slightly to my head: the contradiction slipped out before I could bite it back.
>
> 'But surely,' Greene was saying, 'I remember perfectly. After one of his witnesses refused to talk, Bogart said: "It's feudal."'
>
> 'No. I'm sorry. He didn't say that.' It was too late to stop now, and I continued gently: 'I went to the film just after reading your article and I was waiting for him to say it. But what he really said was "It's futel".'
>
> 'Futel? But what does it mean?'
>
> 'It's how Americans pronounce "futile".'
>
> Greene stared at me for a moment then began to shake with laughter. The fact that he had based a whole careful piece of social criticism on a single misapprehended word seemed to fill him with genuine glee.[5]

Cultural reading and misreading between the discourses of the United States and Britain has been a feature of the English-speaking experience at least since the eighteenth century. But the whole thing has never quite been called off. In fact, by the twentieth century it is at least arguable that this relationship of difference had entered a period of crucial intimacy. Its focal point was undoubtedly 1917.

In April of that year, the intervention of the United States into the war in Europe marked the end of an era. From now on, the New

World would play a decisive role in the affairs of the Old. Indeed, the Old World was in considerable disarray. Revolution filled the air. Empires were crumbling. There had been an uprising in Ireland in the previous year. In Russia, an atmosphere of unrest which had been growing since February climaxed in the Bolshevik uprising of November. Britain was racked by industrial disputes. In May 1917, half the French army, fifty-four divisions, mutinied as a result of the costly offensive mounted by General Nivelle in the previous month. In September, ten thousand Russian troops stationed in Champagne overthrew their officers, organized Soviets, and proclaimed the Bolshevik revolution. And for the British, some very odd developments lay ahead.

The events which took place at the British Army base camp known as the 'Bull Ring', sited at Étaples in France in 1917, have never been officially designated as 'mutiny' and vague accounts of 'unrest' have been used to smother what, in retrospect, seems to have had much in common with developments elsewhere. Military discipline had evidently come perilously close to breakdown. Stories of a growing subterranean, anarchic subculture on the Western Front, with revolutionary bands of deserters wandering amongst the shell holes and ruins of no-man's land, circulated freely. Reinforcements en route to the front had begun to make sardonic noises which sounded suspiciously like the baa-ing of lambs. Infractions of military discipline were violently dealt with at establishments like the Bull Ring, where the punishment for men convicted of desertion or cowardice in the face of the enemy was summary execution. 'Field Punishment No. I', whose victims were spreadeagled on gun carriages for hours at a time, was commonplace. Étaples became a kind of hell on earth. Institutionalized cruelty disguised as 'training' was meted out on a massive scale to men whose sole escape from it lay in a transfer to the killing fields of the front. The poet Wilfred Owen described the scene in a letter to his mother:

> I lay awake in a windy tent in the middle of a vast, dreadful encampment. It seemed neither France nor England, but a kind of paddock where the beasts are kept a few days before the shambles.
> ... I thought of the very strange look on all the faces in that camp; an incomprehensible look, which a man will never see in England; nor can it be seen in any battle. But only in Étaples. It was not despair, or terror, it was more terrible than terror, for it was a blindfold look, and without expression, like a dead rabbit's.[6]

As tension increased throughout the Allied armies, it seemed inevitable that the camp should finally explode in what one commentary calls 'a frantic wild uprising – an eruption that was to turn into six days of open mutiny with 100,000 men immobilized in the vital week before the start of the Passchendaele offensive.'[7]

An account of the sort of treatment that led to the uprising has been given by a 17-year-old soldier who found himself an unwilling member of a firing squad:

> The first man I had to help to kill was a private in my own regiment, the Argyll and Sutherland Highlanders, a fact which filled me with even greater shame. He was said to have fled in the face of the enemy.
>
> We marched to a quarry outside Étaples at first dawn. The victim was brought out from a shed and led struggling to a chair to which he was then bound and a white handkerchief placed over his heart as our target area.
>
> Mortified by the sight of the poor wretch tugging at his bonds, twelve of us, on the order, raised our rifles unsteadily. Some of the men, unable to face the ordeal, had got themselves drunk overnight. They could not have aimed straight if they had tried, and, contrary to popular belief, all twelve rifles were loaded. The condemned man had also been plied with whisky during the night, but he had remained sober through fear.
>
> The tears were rolling down my cheeks as he went on attempting to free himself from the ropes attaching him to the chair. I aimed blindly and when the gunsmoke had cleared away we were further horrified to see that, although wounded, the intended victim was still alive. Still blindfolded, he was attempting to make a run for it still strapped to the chair. The blood was running freely from a chest wound. An officer in charge stepped forward to put the finishing touch with a revolver held to the poor man's temple.
>
> He had only once cried out and that was when he shouted the one word 'mother'. He could not have been very much older than me. We were told later that in fact he had been suffering from shellshock, a condition not recognized by the army in 1917.
>
> By the time I had taken part in four more such dawn executions, I did not have to feign illness. Like the other executioners, I was screaming in my sleep and physically ill every day. I was put into a hospital and strapped down to the bed to prevent me running away. I was then sent away from Étaples and all its horrors to the Italian Front. The simple business of being twice wounded there

was less injurious by far than all the mental scars that Étaples left with me for the rest of my life.[8]

All public executions are, of course, designed not so much to display the power of the state over the body of its members as to reinforce the ineluctable conditions of membership. A military execution crudely simplifies and intensifies that design. In this case, the wretched victim is first bound and then slaughtered in a ritual which serves to reinforce the point that his position is irreversible. As a soldier, he has to confront hostile fire, and no stratagem that he can devise is able to change the situation. The man who is said to have 'fled in the face of the enemy' is simply faced, as a consequence, with a ritualized version of the fire from which he fled. That he tries to 'make a run for it' in the face of the firing squad reinforces the point. In the end, it makes no difference whether he runs towards or away from the enemy or whether the bullets that enter his body are German or British.

However, a major paradox gnaws at this purpose and its symbol is the indifferent bullet. If the victim's execution by firing squad serves to make running away pointless, if any running leads not away from, but only and always towards the guns, then for the victim any distinction between friend and enemy must effectively dissolve. And once that wall has been breached, other vital distinctions supportive of it also collapse. So in the above passage, the executioner's sympathy for the victim slides inexorably into a most subversive identification with him: one in which it is the executioner who is finally incarcerated, 'put into a hospital', and then 'strapped down to the bed to prevent me running away'. In short, the executioner is himself virtually executed. And the 'mental scars' left by that experience behind the lines are then measured against and seen to be no less 'injurious' than the scars of wounds received at the front. In this way, it might be argued that the exertion of maximum discipline – execution by firing squad – inevitably provokes what it seeks to defeat – wholesale mutiny and defection.[9] A wiser society might invest in an opposite course.

The year 1917 was also a year of major cultural revolution, and particularly in the field of popular entertainment. When, acceding to the demands of the United States Navy Department, the City of New Orleans closed down its red light district in November, one immediate effect of the legislation was the migration of jazz music to the large northern cities and thence, in modified form, to the world at large. And this series of events probably made its principal impact on the experience of people in general through the noisy emergence of new forms of public dancing derived from the Africa-inflected southern cultures of the Americas.

An early example of the process and its effects had been the astounding impact of the Argentinian 'tango' on polite European society on the eve of the First World War. Forty years later, Jean Cocteau reflected that he 'could write a chapter on the tango analogous to Michelet's on the café':

> Everyone had gone crazy – this was 1913: Soto and his cousin Manolo Martinez had brought the tango from Argentina, in a gramophone case. They were living in a little private house, in Montmorency. You saw old ladies there who had never before left their own rooms, aristocratic young women slumming: old ones or young would dance glued to Soto or else to Martinez. The tango madness was almost incredible, when you think of it. It marked the downfall of the Faubourg Saint-Germain. It heralded the war. The whole city was dancing the tango, whose steps were very complicated in those days. Huge gentlemen would step gravely in time to the beat, stopping on one leg, lifting the other like a dog taking a piss, exposing the soles of their patent-leather slippers. They plastered down their hair with Argentine lotions. No one paid any attention to age anymore; they just tangoed.[10]

Cocteau sees the tango as a symbol of the disruptive alien forces which 'heralded the war'. They brought the collapse of European social and intellectual hierarchies (those aristocratic young women, the Faubourg Saint-Germain, the distinctions of age) and their replacement by an overwhelming transatlantic brutishness (stopping on one leg, lifting the other like a dog). No wonder the Pope tried to ban it. Similar concerns characterized the response to the impact of North American culture on Europe after the conflict. As the 'jazz age' developed, a series of non-European, even apparently Africa-derived new dances began to epitomize its challenge. To white, European ears, feet, and sensibilities at large, the new rhythms of the music and the movement of bodies it provoked seemed scandalously wild, dangerously libidinous. If some of the implications of the tango had been at least partly obscured by its foreign title, the vey names, let alone the lifted legs of the newest dances – The Grizzly Bear, the Turkey Trot, the Ostrich Walk, the Foxtrot, the Tiger Rag – spoke directly and in English of an untamed, unleashed and undermining animality.

In Europe, the strange music and the disturbing dances which flooded across the Atlantic were part and parcel of an incursion from the New World that was the price of peace, or at least of armistice, in the Old. So amongst the first post-war projects was an undeclared resistance to, or at the least a covert moderation of, that American 'otherness' whose colour was black and whose nature was animal. A programme to tame the invading bears, turkeys, ostriches, tigers and foxes seemed highly desirable, even necessary.

In Britain, a specific domesticating gambit quickly emerged. It involved a characteristic and spectacularly successful policy of incorporation, enlistment and containment, entirely appropriate to – and already a proven success within – an imperial culture. One discourse would, in a mode perfected in the practice of colonial administration, carefully read and painstakingly reinscribe another in a policing exercise of some complexity. The result was the creation of a body known as the Imperial Society of Teachers of Dancing, and the development under its jurisdiction of a mode of bodily movement in ballroom dancing known as the 'English Style'. Successfully exported along the highways of empire, reinforced by a massive programme of intensive instruction, dance-hall building, and the making of records and later radio programmes carefully tailored to its requirements, this became the most influential mode of social dancing in Britain, in the far-flung British Empire, and amongst Europeans in all corners of the world. Its influence on manners, physical comportment, social horizons and expectations, mores, and indeed all the conceivable trajectories of life itself was, and remains, incalculable. Millions of people, currently in middle age or younger, almost literally owe their existence to liaisons contracted at 'dances' held under the influence of the 'English Style'. And, for those millions, if there is one name forever associated with all that 'dancing' of this sort and in that style implies, it is the name of Victor Silvester.

As one of the teachers of modern ballroom dancing officially invested by the Imperial Society of Teachers of Dancing with the responsibility for taming the animality of jazz dance (he was appointed to the committee of the ballroom branch in 1924), Victor Silvester promoted and became identified with a mode of comportment whose vestiges remain with us to this day. In it, a discourse of transatlantic savagery, the Grizzly Bear, the Ostrich Walk, the Turkey Trot, the Tiger Rag, the Foxtrot is translated and mediated – even anglicized – until it subsides into that of the Slow Foxtrot. The frantic gyrations of the Charleston (performed as an exhibitionist, solo spectacle) dwindles into the sedate quickstep, redesigned for couples and danced to what was appropriately labelled a 'strict tempo'. The waltz was resuscitated. Silvester was later instrumental in the importation of similarly tranquillized confections from Latin America. The highly suggestive sexual dimensions of dances such as – above all – the Tango, followed by the Samba, the Rhumba, the Cha-cha-cha were, under his direction, made safe for British Home and Colonial consumption. He finally and famously controlled the music itself, forming his aptly named Strict Tempo Ballroom Orchestra.

Silvester's prestige and influence were astounding. By the time of his death in 1978, his book *Modern Ballroom Dancing* (first published in 1927) had reached its fifty-seventh edition, and had sold over one million copies. His weekly radio broadcasts for the BBC found an enthusiastic reception in every corner of the world. The records made by his Ballroom Orchestra eventually sold more than seventy-five million copies. His precisely clipped and carefully acquired upper-class vowel sounds – inevitably associated with instructions for specific bodily movements in the dance – were uniquely famous and endlessly parodied.[11] It was an astonishing achievement for that young soldier for whom experience as an unwilling member of a firing squad had proved so traumatic.

It would be facile to suggest that Victor Silvester's youthful role as army executioner informed his more mature activities as dance teacher and orchestra leader in other than a metaphorical sense. Yet the metaphor has its appeal. In both these capacities, it could be argued that Silvester acted as an instrument of social control. And the control he exercised – poorly in wartime, with spectacular success in peace – was precisely over the body, coercing it to meet society's exemplary demands. A dance-teacher/band-leader shares with military band leaders and military drill-sergeants the job of imposing regimes of precise, 'strict-tempo' movement on the bodies of groups of human beings. Viewed in this light, the serried ranks of firing-squad and dance-band take on a superficial, if disturbing resemblance.

Dance, it is surely universally recognized, is a fundamental cultural ritual in which the body enacts and reinforces a society's norms, beliefs and taboos, even to the extent, as in Western European and North American societies, of providing the occasions for mating and subsequent propagation. Silvester's unique, and uniquely fore-grounded 'policing' role both as military executioner and dancing master serves to heighten the coercive propensities of social dancing, its operation as a means of compulsion and constraint, and its function as a major site where conflicting forces within a culture's ideology will compete for dominance. It would, of course, be misleading to make too much of the faint military aura that in any case always seemed to invest Silvester's bearing and personality, and ultimately surfaced in and moulded the bodily movements of the style he endorsed. But that it represented at some level a response to the groundswell of his own historical context cannot be doubted. He was named Victor to commemorate a victory in the Boer War announced on the day of his birth, 25 February 1900, and immediately after the First World War he applied to enter the British Officers' Training Establishment at Sandhurst. He was accepted, but left after three weeks to return to London as a dance teacher.[12] This military dimension lends an odd symbolic force to the notion that social dancing was a central area in which the meaningful form of some of the twentieth-century's major cultural and economic en- counters – between America and Europe for instance – was negotiated. Indeed, it makes it possible to see as a quasi-military engagement a process that our ideology seeks to nominate as an amiable 'special' relationship of quite another kind. The two poles, war and affection, military marching and lover's dalliance, coexist and coalesce in that relationship's history much as they do in a popular dance-hall song of the period called, appropriately, 'Sweet- hearts on Parade':

> Two by Two, they go Marching through
> The Sweethearts on Parade
> I sit and pine, to join their Line,
> The Sweethearts on Parade.
> I'd love to join their fun, but they bar me,
> It takes more than one to join their army

But for a monument genuinely appropriate to that cultural battle, we would have to look no further than the phrase which, more than any other, still conjures up the name of Victor Silvester and his role for millions of people. For more than fifty years this son of the Vicar of Wembley was one of the most influential means by which American culture in the early twentieth century was 'read', filtered and moulded until it assumed a shape acceptable to British pre- suppositions. The only fitting memorial for him must be the instructional formula he made so famous. As its five words of command unroll, encased in their cut-glass English military accent, a challenging and African/American commitment to volatility, speed and life, is safely policed, cushioned and contained by a British/ European insistence on a style of bodily movement whose watchwords are those of moderation, deliberation and control:

'slow, slow, quick quick, slow'. In this 'strict tempo', British culture stepped tentatively onto the floor of the modern world.

You came a long way from St Louis

Of course, the discursive terrains of that world continued to be shaped by other events. Two of the most significant of them also took place in the year 1917. First was the founding of the University of Cambridge Tripos (i.e. degree) in English, which effectively established in Britain the study of the subject as we know it to this day. The second event was also a literary one: the publication of T. S. Eliot's highly influential volume of verse *Prufrock and Other Observations*. In fact, the impact and influence, if not the content, of the latter could be said to be a direct result of the former, for the professional teachers of the new subject quickly found in Eliot a poetic stance to match their critical presuppositions.[13] The fact that Eliot was not English was usually ignored. His voice somehow seemed to speak from the centre.

He had virtually danced his way there. In June 1913, the year before his appointment to the Sheldon Travelling Fellowship at Harvard which made his momentous trip to Oxford and London possible, we find Eliot paying a fee of seven dollars to one Emma Wright Gibbs for three hours' dancing lessons.[14] The investment paid off. In mid-Atlantic in July 1914, he reports that 'we have great fun, especially when it comes to dancing to the sound of the captain's phonograph'.[15] Yet his trip to Europe was also moving him away from the American fountainhead. At Oxford in November of that year, he confesses to being 'as much *au courant* of Cambridge [Massachusetts] life as anyone can who has not yet learned the fox trot', and resolves that, when he returns, he will put himself in the hands of a local dance teacher 'for a month of the strictest training'. The new style of ballroom dancing, he jocularly but accurately calculates, is after all one of the spearheads of the American cultural penetration of Europe.

> I was able to make use of the fox trot in a debate in the college common room a few evenings ago. The subject was ' Resolved that this society abhors the threatened Americanisation of Oxford'. I supported the negative: I pointed out to them frankly how much they owed to Amurrican culcher in the drayma (including the movies) in music, in the cocktail, and in the dance. And see, said I, what we the few Americans here are losing while we are bending

our energies toward your uplift . . . we the outposts of progress are compelled to remain in ignorance of the fox trot. You will be interested to hear that my side won the debate by two votes.'[16]

Eliot soon learned to foxtrot. Better still, he soon learned that his transatlantic dancing style offered a highly successful means of access to the social as well as the intellectual life of London. It was his entrée to the city:

I have been mostly among poets and artists, but I have also met a few ladies, and have even danced. The large hotels have dances on Saturday nights, to which one can go by paying or by taking dinner there. By being admitted to two dancing parties I have met several English girls, mostly about my own age, and especially two who are very good dancers.[17]

But to Eliot, the character of English intellectual life was perhaps mirrored by its wooden social rituals:

The English style of dancing is very stiff and old fashioned, and I terrified one poor girl (she is Spanish at that) by starting to dip in my one-step.[18]

Nevertheless, by 1915, the American 'dip' – together with the new spectacle of women smoking – were, as he recognized, the outward manifestations of a bewildering modernity:

Miss Nancy Ellicott smoked
And danced all the modern dances;
And her aunts were not quite sure how they felt about it,
But they knew that it was modern.

('Cousin Nancy')[19]

And in the same year, he found himself a willing agent of this transatlantic mode in his forays into the favours of young women in wartime London:

The two I mentioned are more adaptable, and caught the American style very quickly. As they are emancipated Londoners I have been out to tea or dinner with them several times, and find them quite different from anything I have known at home or here . . . They are charmingly sophisticated (even 'disillusioned') without being hardened; and I confess to taking great pleasure in seeing women smoke, though for that matter I do not know any English girls who do not.[20]

There can be no doubt that the representative of the American style found one of his dancing encounters to be momentous at a number of levels:

> These English girls have such amusing names – I have met two named 'Phyllis' – and one named 'Vivien'.[21]

Subsequent glimpses of Eliot and his new wife Vivien often present them as dancers:

> in these early days, when Vivienne [*sic*] still enjoyed bouts of good health and high spirits, they could occasionally afford to take an evening off, or a Sunday afternoon. They rolled up the rug, put a record on the gramophone, and danced.[22]

In March 1919, Eliot writes to Mary Hutchinson,

> Vivien says she is lunching with you on Thursday. Won't you come on later (at 5.45) and dance at a place near Baker Street. They teach the new dances and steps, which I don't know and want to learn. I hope you won't mind my being rather out of date.[23]

Lyndall Gordon reports how 'Eliot and his wife used to foxtrot, very solemnly, in the twenties' and perhaps aspects of this are reflected in one of the short stories Vivien wrote for *The Criterion* in 1924, under the *nom de plume* of 'Feiron Morris'.[24] Entitled *Thé Dansant*, it certainly catches something of the impact of the new American (North or South) dancing on a duller European tradition. It may even offer a brief but provocative glimpse of a slightly disguised Eliot himself. Sibylla, as caged and as representative of death in life as her namesake at Cumae in the epigraph to *The Waste Land*, finds her attention drawn to a specific figure at a tea dance. Tall, thin-faced, and clearly not English, he moves in a distinctive and intriguing manner. Unlike the shabby, awkward English couples, thoughtlessly clumping right across the dance-floor, this man covers only a small area, but does so with considerable grace and deliberation. Sibylla immediately classifies him as American or Argentinian. In her view, he is the only person in the room who could be said to be genuinely dancing. For her, it is made clear, the word 'dancer' virtually connotes an exotic American culture.[25]

The degree to which Eliot himself could in more general terms be said to cover very little ground and to take a long time about it abides our question. But the image of a barely tamed transatlantic animality, embodied in Argentinian tango or American jazz, and bringing life to a dead European landscape, sets off familiar echoes. And Eliot certainly never ceased to see American dancing as quite distinct from that of Europe. T. S. Matthews describes how, many years on

> when Eliot was guest of honour at a literary society dinner at Cambridge, he was heard explaining to the High Table that because of the Negro influence in American music, no American could waltz properly and no Englishman could really foxtrot.[26]

Eliot's lengthy, tragic foxtrot with Vivien was ultimately to prove an almost wholly disastrous venture. But whatever its consequences, on a personal and emotional level its limits hardly rest there. For in its macrocosmic dimension as a symbolic encounter between American and British, New World and Old World culture, its implications never ceased to haunt central areas of his work.

Brush up your Shakespeare

A good deal of that work involved a preliminary clearing of ground. Once ensconced in Britain, Eliot had set about the traditional American task of explaining his hosts' history and culture to them. Oxford persuaded him that he 'must learn to talk English' and he became convinced, in terms of literary culture at least, that the English had got things lamentably wrong and that the situation required positive action.[27] Writing to Richard Aldington in 1921, he explicitly announces

> my general programme of literary criticism which must by this time be fairly obvious to you, and I hope and believe fairly congenial: I mean that any innuendos I make at the expense of Milton, Keats, Shelley and the nineteenth century in general are part of a plan to help us rectify, so far as *I* can, the immense skew in public opinion toward our pantheon of literature.[28]

Although the 32-year-old American fails to make entirely clear to whom the key terms 'us' and 'our' refer in this project, its political dimension is evident enough in its systematic relegation of the revolutionary impulses embodied in the work of Milton and the Romantic poets, and its later promotion of an alternative conservative tradition involving Donne and the 'Metaphysical' poets. In respect of the key figure of Shakespeare, a completely new 'rectifying' choreography becomes evident. The modern cultural dance Eliot was proposing would require the downgrading of *Hamlet* and the elevation of another work.

Even today this seems an astonishing judgement, certainly one which strikes an unrepentant 'foreign' note. And although E. M. Forster decided that the essay which embodies it, 'Hamlet and his problems' (1919), belonged with those of Eliot's works whose difficulties are largely our own fault, we might well feel that his conclusion that the bulk of Eliot's work 'has nothing to do with the English tradition in literature, or law, or order' finds confirmation here.[29] Be that as it may, Eliot seems to have decided that Hamlet's anguished struggle with an inherited order of being could in no circumstances be presumed to reflect or to speak for the Britain he thought he had found. Even the wretched class-racked Prufrock was not Prince Hamlet, nor was he meant to be.

Thus the essay 'Hamlet and his problems' famously dismisses the play as 'most certainly an artistic failure' owing to its incapacity to realize 'intractable' material. It contains 'superfluous and inconsistent scenes' and 'both workmanship and thought are in an unstable position' throughout. It is 'the "Mona Lisa" of literature'. Apparently, Shakespeare had here 'tackled a problem which proved too much for him'.[30]

By comparison, and surprisingly, the culmination of Shakespeare's 'tragic successes' turns out to be *Coriolanus*. Although this play may not be as 'interesting' as *Hamlet*, 'it is, with *Antony and Cleopatra*, Shakespeare's most assured artistic success', a consummate masterpiece, 'intelligible, self-complete, in the sunlight'. To the extent that this seems to contradict a 'standard' response to Shakespeare's tragedies, and despite Eliot's disingenuous semi-recantation fourteen years later ('my words were even interpreted as maintaining that *Coriolanus* is a greater play than *Hamlet*') a particular reading of *Coriolanus* – and by extension a specific re-mapping of the Shakespearean canon – is obviously at stake here.[31]

Its roots go deep. In his early engagements with Shakespeare, Eliot seemed to support the claims of the so-called 'disintegrators', such as J. M. Robertson. Grounding their work in historical and textual analysis, they denied that the plays were the work of a single, unified author. 'Hamlet and his problems' confirms the point explicitly:

> Mr. Robertson points out, very pertinently, how critics have failed in their 'interpretation' of *Hamlet* by ignoring what ought to be very obvious: that *Hamlet* is a stratification, that it represents the efforts of a series of men, each making what he could out of the work of his predecessors.

But later – after some hesitation he tells us – Eliot is persuaded to accept the critic G. Wilson Knight's notion of a 'spatial' interpretation of Elizabethan drama, appropriate to Shakespeare, in which a 'centred' and unified author emerges as the source and guarantee of the gigantic unity of 'vision' expressed by the plays. 'Interpretation' for Knight involves the translation of an original imaginative response to the play into the 'slower consciousness of logic and intellect':

> It is exactly this translation from one order of consciousness to another that interpretation claims to perform. Uncritically, and passively, it receives the whole of the poet's vision; it then proceeds to re-express this experience in its own terms.
>
> To receive the whole Shakespearean vision into the intellectual consciousness demands a certain and very definite act of mind. One must be prepared to see the whole play in space as well as time.[32]

In the event, such an intense attention to the 'spatial' dimension effectively undermines attention to that of time. The one cannot simply be responded to 'as well as' the other: these are quite distinct planes of experience and when he finally does bring himself to accept the spatial interpretation of Shakespeare ('It has taken me a long time to recognize the justification of what Mr. Wilson Knight calls "interpretation" ' he writes in his Introduction to *The Wheel of Fire*), Eliot effectively denies himself the temporal one. J. M. Robertson's disintegrative, historical and thus essentially temporal mode of analysis is abandoned in favour of Knight's unifying a-historical and 'spatial' commitment to a single Bard's coherent 'vision'.[33]

Hugh Grady has argued that such a decision in effect confirmed Eliot's continuing involvement with the Romantic roots feeding the Symbolism and the Modernism to which he was drawn. The hermeneutics at stake were committed to a unified, synchronic, spatial dimension in art, at the expense of a disunified, diachronic or temporal dimension. For 'spatialization' brings with it not only a notion of the author's unity, but a reinforced sense of the text's autonomy and an insistence on its separation from its own social and cultural context.

Grady has rightly drawn attention to the 'naïve underestimation of historical difference' characteristic of Knight's Shakespearean criticism, and he points out the extent to which this 'lack of historical consciousness fits in with the whole project of a spatial hermeneutics, as a part of the Modernist revolt against nineteenth century time and preoccupation with history.'[34] In Grady's words, 'The revolt against time in the arts was a deeply felt revolt against history': a history that, by the time of the First World War, had produced, not progress and enlightenment, but catastrophe and monstrosity.³⁵ For all its professed interest in the past and in 'tradition', Eliot's Modernism shares these characteristics. In short, as part of its commitment to the identification and transmission of an inherited culture, it smuggles in a suspicion and finally a suppression of history. For Eliot, 'tradition' becomes a device for the interdiction of time.

Eliot's commitment to a revision and a rewriting of British literary history in order to promote John Donne and the Metaphysical poets is in one sense its monument. In presenting these authors as Modernists *avant la lettre*, separated from us by the only-now-discernible tragedy of a 'dissociation of sensibility', he effectively proposed our underlying continuity, unity and finally identity with them across the years. They were as English forebears are to certain modern Americans: traceable, palpable, reachable ancestors, whose blood runs commonly in veins on both sides of the Atlantic. To recognize them is to leap that ocean, to dissolve those years, to eradicate that difference and to drain away the history that produces it.

We have seen that a major casualty of this process in respect of Shakespeare's plays must, almost inevitably, be *Hamlet*. That play's roots in aspects of its own distinctive culture, its deployment of particular beliefs, rituals, relationships and motifs, such as those of incest and revenge, that seem specific to its own way of life, will render it in Eliot's terms so 'foreign' as to be un-recuperable. That culture's difference from our own will always thrust an unassimilable dimension of time between itself and our efforts to embrace it. Eliot even goes so far as to argue that *Hamlet*'s own history misleads us. As a result, *Coriolanus* appears to him to be a much more obvious candidate for the accolade of 'masterpiece'. Here the Modernist embracing of 'spatial interpretation', with its implications of transcendence and universal applicability, will suggest the play as a model for both personal and national experience. Indeed, the play might even, as a result, prove able to take on a heroic dimension, become capable of dealing with aspects of a universal, transhistorical human predicament.

The Eagle Rock

The absolute union of body and mind, intellect and physical form, has been imagined most powerfully in our century as a kind of prelapsarian, perfect, and 'timeless' mode of being to which humans are effortlessly born, but from which in the post-Renaissance world they have sadly declined. The seventeenth-century's supposed realization of this condition has been felt, by both Modernists and Symbolists, to offer a standard by which the nature of the modern situation may be judged. The ideal appears fully-fledged in Donne's account of Elizabeth Drury;

> Her pure and eloquent blood
> Spoke in her cheeks, and so distinctly wrought,
> That one might almost say, her body thought.

Symbolist writers in particular have frequently tended to propose the dance as an image of this ideal fusion of the physical and the intellectual, body and mind. For French Symbolist poets, the dancer presented a spectacle in which form and meaning could be said to be finally identical, and Mallarmé wrote a lengthy account in this vein of Loïe Fuller, the American dancer, whose performances in Paris at the *Folies Bergère* seemed to encapsulate the transcendent essence of poetry itself – something perhaps best described in the Symbolist mode in English by Arthur Symons who stresses the non-discursive nature of dance, claiming that in it 'Nothing is stated, there is no intrusion of words used for the irrelevant purpose of describing . . . and the dancer, with her gesture, all pure symbol, evokes, from her mere beautiful motion, idea, sensation, all that one need ever to know of event.'[36]

As Frank Kermode has pointed out, Yeats's poem 'Michael Robartes and the Dancer' alludes significantly to this sort of view when it depicts the dragon killed by the knight who loves the lady as that capacity for abstract rational thinking which is distracting her from her true love:

>   it's plain
> The half-dead dragon was her thought,
> That every morning rose again
> And dug its claws and shrieked and fought.[37]

What is true of women in particular is also the case with human beings in general, so Yeats's notion goes. The development of mind independently of the body strikes him as a modern disaster. Its source lies in the Renaissance, when the possibility of a human unity of being first began to disintegrate. Eliot, of course, was later to develop this notion in his idea of a crucial cultural lapse, a catastrophic 'dissociation of sensibility' which supposedly took place in the seventeenth century.

Yeats's constantly reiterated symbol for the condition available before the catastrophe is that of the female dancer, a creature in whose art body and soul, physical being and intellect, form and content, all merge to achieve the perfect, timeless, indivisible coherence commemorated in his own lines

> O body swayed to music, O brightening glance,
> How can we know the dancer from the dance?
> ('Among School Children')

Kermode has pointed out that, amongst his otherwise rather eccentric choices for the *Oxford Book of Modern Verse* (1936), Yeats included a number of poems such as W. J. Turner's 'The Dancer',

> The young girl dancing lifts her face
> Passive among the drooping flowers;
> The jazz band clatters sticks and bones
> In a bright rhythm through the hours.

in which the dancer's expressionless visage gives a positive indication that the mind, whose dominance is usually manifested in an alertness of the eyes, is subjugated to and satisfactorily merged with the moving body:

> But Saturn has not that strange look
> Unhappy, still, and far away,
> As though upon the face of Night
> Lay the bright wreck of day.

The same is true of another selection: Joseph Campbell's poem, also called 'The Dancer':

> His face is a mask
> It is so still and white:
> His withered eyes shut,
> Unmindful of light.

As an example of the opposite, of the 'dissociated' time-ridden incoherence characteristic of modern life, Yeats points to the figure of an international statesman, President Woodrow Wilson, and in particular to his eyes:

The men that Titian painted, the men that Jongsen painted, even the men of Van Dyck, seemed at moments like great hawks at rest. In the Dublin National Gallery there hung, perhaps still hang, upon the same wall, a portrait of some Venetian gentleman by Strozzi, and Mr. Sargent's painting of President Wilson. Whatever thought broods in the dark eyes of that Venetian gentleman has drawn its life from his whole body; it feeds upon it as the flame feeds upon the candle – and should the thought be changed, his pose would change, his very cloak would rustle for his whole body thinks. President Wilson lives only in the eyes, which are steady and intent; the flesh about the mouth is dead, and the hands are dead, and the clothes suggest no movement of his body nor any movement but that of the valet, who has brushed and folded in mechanical routine. There all was an energy flowing outward from the nature itself; here all is the anxious study and slight deflection of external force; there man's mind and body were predominantly subjective; here all is objective, using those words not as philosophy uses them, but as we use them in conversation.[38]

A Symbolist's reference to an international political figure, involved in – and broken by – affairs of state, war, and the pressures of power might serve to bring us back to *Coriolanus*. But oddly enough, so might those remarks about thinking with the body, and allied to them, the notion of dancing. For, surprisingly, a notion of dancing haunts *Coriolanus* at a profound, barely articulated level. In what is clearly the source material for the bulk of the play, Plutarch's *Lives of Noble Grecians and Romanes* (1579), the rambling account of the 'Life of Caius Martius Coriolanus' tells of the 'uprore and discord, the nobilitie against the communalitie' that took place in Rome following Coriolanus's condemnation and banishment. Amongst a number of strange 'sightes and wonders' reported to the Senate at that time was one in which a man called Titus Latinus – stricken with a kind of paralysis – claimed that Jupiter had appeared to him in a dream

and commaunded him to signifie to the Senate, that they had caused a very vile lewde daunser to goe before the procession.

After reporting his vision, Latinus's paralysis immediately vanished. The Senate's inquiries into Jupiter's displeasure revealed that there was indeed a basis for the complaint. One citizen had recently commanded that a bondman of his who had offended him should be publicly whipped 'up and down the market place' and afterwards killed.

and as they had him in execution, whipping him cruelly, they dyd so martyre the poore wretch, that for the cruell smarte and payne he felt, he turned and writhed his bodie, in straunge and pitiefull sorte. The procession by chaunce came by even at the same time, and many that followed it, were hartely moved and offended with the sight, saying: that this was no good sight to behold, nor mete to be met in procession time. . .

Now when *Latinus* had made reporte to the Senate of the vision that had happened to him, they were devising whom this unpleasaunt daunser should be, that went before the procession. Therupon certain that stoode by, remembred the poore slave that was so cruelly whipped through the market place, whom they afterwardes put to death: and the thing that made them remember it, was the straunge and rare manner of his punishment. The priestes hereupon were repaired unto for their advise: they were wholly of opinion, that it was the whipping of the slave. So they caused the slaves master to be punished, and beganne againe a new procession, & all other showes and sightes in honour of *Jupiter*.[39]

Plutarch takes the moral of this savage story to be that the people are commanded 'wholy to dispose themselves to serve God, leaving all other busines and matters a side'. And in respect of Coriolanus, the implication is, clearly enough, that he is the castigated servant of the state whose inappropriate punishment turns him metaphorically into the 'vile, lewd dancer' whose appalling gyrations distract the citizens from their proper duties to the gods. In short, the banishment and ultimate destruction of Coriolanus is presented here as a cruel and ultimately self-undermining indulgence on Rome's part.

Although the play's direct involvement with this part of Plutarch's account is limited to one or two instances (e.g. IV, vi, 60–1), the material at large has evidently been received and internalized on some troubled frequency. In any case, this story of cruel execution and civic self-indulgence makes a decisive connection with issues current in the early seventeenth century, through its affecting central image. The very terms 'vile', 'lewd' and 'unpleasaunt' used in respect of a 'daunser' signal a precise frame of discursive reference and an area of specific concern.

The early modern debate about dancing has its roots in Plato's *Laws*, and they stretch through Lucian of Somosata's dialogue on 'The Dance', to Sir Thomas Elyot's *The Boke Named The Governour* (1531), Sir John Davies's poem 'Orchestra' (1596) and Robert Burton's *The Anatomy of Melancholy* (1621). In that debate, two irreconcilable notions confront each other.

Objections to dancing as vile and lewd, involving personal gratification to the level of debauchery, go back well before those of the Puritans. An example is Barclay's translation of Sebastian Brandt's *The Ship of Fools* (1509):

What els is daunsynge but euen a nurcery
Or els a bayte to purchase and meyntayne
In yonge hertis the vyle synne of rybawdry
Them fetrynge therin, as in a dedely chayne
And to say trouth in wordes clere and playne
Venereous people haue all theyr hole pleasaunce
Theyre vyce to norysshe by this vnthryfty daunce.

And wanton people disposyd vnto syn
To satysfye theyr mad concupyscence
With hasty cours vnto this daunsynge ryn
To seke occasyon of vyle synne and offence
And to expresse my mynde in short sentence
This vycioцe game oft tymes doth attyse
By his lewde synes, chast hartis vnto vyce.

After indulging 'theyr will and theyr pleasaunce', such 'lewde' dancers then fall 'to great mysgouernaunce' – something which guarantees their place on the 'Ship of Fools'.[40]

Predictably, numerous Puritan pamphlets denounce dancing. Salome's dance before Herod offers a paradigm for bodily movement which, in John Northbrooke's terms, should be seen as 'not lawfull nor tollerable, but wicked and filthie'. Philip Stubbes characterizes dancing in his *The Anatomy of Abuses* (1583) as 'an introduction to whordom, a preparative to wantonnes, a provocative to uncleanes, & an introite to al kind of lewdenes', and the diatribes culminate in Prynne's commentary in *Histriomastix* which concludes that 'our theatrical amorous mixt lascivious dancing, is sinfull and unchristian at the last, if not HEATHENISH AND DIABOLICALL.'[41]

But there was another notion of dancing apparently sanctioned by the Bible: the dancing of the Israelites to celebrate their release from Egypt, David's dancing before the Ark, the dancing of Jephthah's daughter, or that of Judith celebrating her conquest of Holofernes. Dancing of this kind could be linked with that praised and commended by Plato and Lucian, which symbolically and publicly enacted the civic virtues, and which is recommended by them as a necessary element in a complete education. In Lucian's dialogue, the figure of Lycinus urgently seeks to persuade Crato of dancing's value in terms of 'culture and instruction':

> it imports harmony into the souls of its beholders, exercising them in what it is fair to see, entertaining them with what it is good to hear, and displaying to them the joint beauty of soul and body.[42]

This is the spirit in which Elizabethan defences of dancing were conceived, but with a specific social and political dimension added to the concepts of harmony and order. For instance, in *The Boke Named The Governour* (1531), Sir Thomas Elyot is careful to distinguish 'lasciuiouse' dancing of a decadent, personal and physical cast,

> suche daunsis whiche (as I late saide) were superstitious and contained in them a spice of idolatrie, or els dyd with unclene motions of countinances irritate the myndes of the dauncers to venereall lustes, whereby fornication and auoutrie were daily increased.[43]

from those more symbolic, public and political forms whose bodily movements symbolize and enact social and moral concord together with the civic virtues appropriate to men and women's divinely ordained natures:

> It is diligently to be noted that the associatinge of man and woman in daunsing, they bothe obseruinge one nombre and tyme in their meuynges, was nat begonne without a speciall consideration, as well for the necessarye coniunction of those two persones, as for the intimation of sondry vertues, whiche be by them represented. And for as moche as by the association of a man and a woman in daunsinge may be signified matrimonie, I coulde in declarynge the dignitie and commoditie of that sacrament make intiere volumes. . . . In euery daunse, of a most auncient custome, there daunseth to gether a man and a woman, holding eche other by the hande or the arme, which betokeneth concorde . . .
>
> A man in his natural perfection is fiers, hardy, stronge in opinion, couaitouse of glorie, desirous of knowledge, appetiting by generation to brynge forth his semblable. The good nature of a woman is to be milde, timerouse, tractable, benigne, of sure remembrance, and shamfast. Diuers other qualities of eche of them moughte be founde out, but these be moste apparaunt, and for this time sufficient.
>
> Wherfore, when we beholde a man and a woman daunsinge to gether, let us suppose there to be a concorde of all the saide qualities, being ioyned to gether, as I have set them in ordre. And the meuing of the man wolde be more vehement, of the woman more delicate, and with lasse aduauncing of the body, signifienge the courage and strenthe that oughte to be in a man, and the pleasant sobreness that shulde be in a woman. And in this wise *fiersenesse* ioyned with *mildenesse* maketh *Seueritie*; *Audacitie* with *timerositie* maketh *Magnanimitie*; wilfull opinion and *Tractabilitie*

(which is to be shortly persuaded and meued) makethe *Constance* a vertue; *Couaitise of Glorie*, adourned with *benignitie* causeth honour; *desire of knowlege* with *sure remembrance* procureth *Sapience*; *Shamfastnes* ioyned to *Appetite of generation* maketh *Continence*, whiche is a meane betwene *Chastitie* and *inordinate luste*. These qualities, in this wise beinge knitte to gether, and signified in the personages of man and woman daunsinge, do expresse or sette out the figure of very nobilitie; which in the higher astate it is contained, the more excellent is the vertue in estimation.[44]

Elyot's presentation of masculinity here obviously matches the stereotypical and patriarchal notion of 'manliness' to which Corio-lanus aspires. Indeed, it may hint at the possibility of inserting that play into the debate about bodily display which, according to John Drakakis, became from the 1580s onwards 'the focus of a politico-religious conflict which centred on the question of sabbatarianism'.[45] This ideal vision of masculinity is linked to and reinforced by dancing of a particular 'public' sort. Its formal movement serves to reinforce the very basis of the society's way of life. It maintains and augments established gender roles by balancing the characteristics supposedly clustering around the poles of 'man' and 'woman' – courage and sobriety, fierceness and mildness, audacity and 'timerositie' – and it proposes a productive mediation between them which generates the most desirable of social modes such as severity, magnanimity, continence and constancy.

Similar concerns activate Sir John Davies's 'Poeme of Dauncing' entitled 'Orchestra'. Here the importuning of Penelope focuses on the function of the dance, considering whether it serves as an inducement to personal lust or as an 'authenticall and laudable' if nonetheless symbolical reinforcement of the movements of the universe at large. The opposition between a kind of 'individual' dancing, which invokes and encourages 'frenzie' and 'rage', and a 'public' sort, which is the very origin of cosmic order, is cleverly exploited in the poem by Antinous:

> DAUNCING (bright Lady) then began to be
> When the first seedes whereof the world did spring,
> The Fire, Ayre, Earth and Water did agree,
> By Love's perswasion, Nature's mighty King,
> To leave their first disordred combating,
> And in a dance such measure to observe,
> As all the world their motion should preserve.
>
> (Stanza 17)[46]

A distinction between the dancing of bestial savagery and a recognizably human 'civill forme of dancing' capable of acting as a means of social maintenance and control is emphatically driven home. Indeed, dancing of this latter sort offers a metaphor for society itself:

> Concords true picture shineth in thys Art,
> Where divers men and women ranked be,
> And every one doth daunce a severall part,
> Yet all as one, in measure doe agree,
> Observing perfect uniformitie:
> All turne together, all together trace,
> And all together honor and embrace.
>
> (Stanza 110)

Many commentators have pointed out that *Coriolanus* repeatedly focuses on the body, draws attention to its capacities as a communicative instrument and, in a play crucially concerned with a notion of the state as a 'body politic', makes the body a reiterated element of metaphor. Menenius's narration of the fable of the rebellion of the 'body's members' against the belly is highlighted within minutes of the play's beginning. Threats to the 'navel of the state' (III, i, 122) are spoken of. The people appear as 'this bosom multiplied' (III, i, 130). The tribunes become the people's 'multitudinous tongue' (III, i, 155), their 'mouths' who should rule their 'teeth' (III, i, 35). A citizen is mocked as 'the great toe of this assembly' (I, i, 154), Coriolanus is a gangrenous 'foot' (III, i, 304) and his banishment ensures that war flows as a laxative within 'the bowels of ungrateful Rome' (IV, v, 131). His dismissal of his enemies as mere bodies 'whose loves I prize / As the dead carcasses of unburied men' (III, iii, 122) finds its echo in a spectacularly physical ending to the play, when Aufidius literally stands on Coriolanus's mutilated body to make his final speech.[47]

Plutarch's account of the Rome of Coriolanus makes no bones about that state's sense that its writ extended fully to the body of its citizens, particularly the poor:

> And suche as had nothing left, their bodyes were layed hold of, and they were made their bonde men, notwithstanding all the woundes and cuttes they shewed, which they had recyved in many battells, fighting for defence of their countrie and common wealth[48]

And the degree to which such authority was woven into language itself by means of names 'derived of some marke or misfortune of the bodie: as *Sylla*, to saye, crooked nosed: *Niger*, blacke: *Rufus*, red: *Caecus* blinde: *Claudus*, lame' is, of course, of particular interest in this play in which the symbolic disclosure of bodily wounds has such an important role.[49] For the fact is that however strongly he clings to an emblematic notion of the body's function in the 'public' mode that physical display such as the 'civill forme of dancing' would endorse, Coriolanus nevertheless finds himself in the same situation as the bond man whom Titus Latinus describes to the Senate in Plutarch's account: he is required to appear as a 'lewd' dancer in a 'personal' or individual mode, bending his body to the citizens' desires in order to win their approval. Rome claims the body that it names. Coriolanus's acceptance of his own nomenclature requires him to wear the 'gown of humility' (II, iii, 41), the 'wolvish toge' (II, iii, 114) or the sheep's clothing. But he must also 'by my body's action teach my mind / A most inherent baseness' (III, ii, 120ff.). He must, in short, offer a seductive public display of his body, flaunt his wounds, perform – as he sees it – a kind of salacious 'dance' in which he seeks to 'practise the insinuating nod' (II, iii, 99) doffing his hat and 'waving' his head in accordance with his mother's advice:

> I prithee now, my son,
> Go to them, with this bonnet in thy hand,
> And thus far having stretched it – here be with them –
> Thy knee bussing the stones – for in such business
> Action is eloquence, and the eyes of th'ignorant
> More learned than the ears – waving thy head,
> Which often, thus, correcting thy stout heart,
> Now humble as the ripest mulberry
> That will not hold the handling
>
> (III, ii, 73ff.)

When he finally agrees to adopt such a role, he does so in a 'harlot's spirit' whose pervading 'lewdness' demeans a voice and body now, as he sees it, given over to mincing mimicry:

> Well I must do't.
> Away my disposition, and possess me
> Some harlot's spirit! My throat of war be turn'd,
> Which choired with my drum, into a pipe
> Small as an eunuch, or the virgin voice
> That babies lull asleep! The smiles of knaves
> Tent in my cheeks, and schoolboys' tears take up

> The glasses of my sight! A beggar's tongue
> Make motion through my lips, and my arm'd knees
> Who bow'd but in my stirrup, bend like his
> That hath received an alms!
>
> (III, ii, 110–20.)

Here Comes the Bride

The sense that an intimacy with *Coriolanus* permeates Eliot's poetry derives from the frequency with which references to it peep through its lines, from the jaunty asseveration of 'A Cooking Egg';

> I shall not want Honour in Heaven
> For I shall meet Sir Philip Sidney
> And have talk with Coriolanus
> And other heroes of that kidney.

to the portentous symbolism of the 'broken Coriolanus' imprisoned by the arrogance of his individualism in *The Waste Land* (l. 415). But one of the most provocative of the play's appearances in Eliot's work occurs in a little-known poem entitled simply 'Ode', printed in the volume *Ara Vos Prec* (1920), and later inexplicably suppressed by him.

'Ode' has an epigraph taken directly from *Coriolanus*:

> To you particularly, and to all the Volscians
> Great hurt and mischief.

The apparently aggressive and menacing nature of these lines is somewhat mitigated when the words are placed in a fuller context, although Eliot significantly fails to supply it. In the play, the passage is uttered by Coriolanus, explaining his name to his former enemies and almost apologizing for the harm he has done to them:

> My name is Caius Martius, who hath done
> To thee particularly, and to all the Volsces,
> Great hurt and mischief: thereto witness may
> My surname, Coriolanus.
>
> (IV, v, 66–9)

In Eliot's typescript a date, Independence Day, 4 July 1918, is included as part of the title. Various assessments of the poem's quality have been made, together with a number of interpretations of its meaning.[50] These usually link it with his marriage to Vivien. Eliot's omission of the full context of the epigraph certainly lends the whole an obscurely threatening air. And the implied violence of some of its images does seem to carry disturbing, if unfocused implications for Eliot's personal life in which Vivien seems to dwindle into a torturing reminder of his regrettable ballroom prowess, the demeaning physicality which it served, and the shaming inadequacies it subsequently revealed.

However, perhaps the link with Vivien exists on a different level from that presupposed by such readings. It is important not to elide the precise significance of its date. In London, Thursday 4 July 1918 was pronounced by *The Times* to be 'one of the great landmarks of history'. The United States had entered the war on the Allied side on Good Friday, 6 April 1917. Fifteen months later, with American troops now established in France and with victory apparently in sight, the celebration of American Independence Day took on an 'Anglo-American' fervour that masked larger ironies of the situation. There was much talk of 'Anglo-Saxon unity'. Messages reporting 'a new and special heartiness' were exchanged between the British and American governments. The King attended a specially arranged baseball match between United States forces in London. A special meeting of the Anglo-Saxon Fellowship took place at Central Hall, Westminster, and was addressed by the Bishop of London. And an editorial in *The Times* thundered in support of what it termed 'the old Anglo-Saxon "world idea"'.[51]

Eliot's 'Ode' clearly refers to the defloration of a bride. But the poem's date and its epigraph place the 'marriage' involved in a broader and more overtly political context than that of Eliot's relationship with Vivien. In February 1917, Eliot had confided to his father that 'If [America] put an army into the field . . . I should have to think over my position carefully.'[52] But whilst Vivien remarks on the 'dreadful effect' war has on the characters of young and old, Eliot seems, when the time came, to have been in favour of Woodrow Wilson's decision to involve the United States.[53] Indeed, he appears to see in the war the possibility of cementing a relationship between America and Britain whose foundations already lie deep. In an (unsigned) review of H. Wilson Harris's *President Wilson: His Problems and His Policy* in the *New Statesman*, he stresses the apparent Anglophilia of the President and former academic, underlining its significance for the strength of an alliance between the two countries, and even making the point that

Friends of an Anglo-American Alliance will be interested to know that Wilson's reforms at Princeton University were largely upon English lines and that his theory of the relation of President and Cabinet has looked towards English models.[54]

By July 1918, the discourse of a warlike Anglo-American unity was well established. On 4 July, *The Times* reported the gratifying naming of the 'Avenue de Président Wilson' in Paris and announced that it was prepared to recognize the dispatch of over a million American troops to Europe as 'the greatest event of modern times'. On the same day, the paper gave full coverage to a speech by the Archbishop of York in which he proposed that the British should

> see in every American whom we may meet one link in the chain which binds the two nations together. 'We cannot escape history.'

Whether Vivien Haigh-Wood saw her own personal relationship to her American husband in that apocalyptic light is unclear. But the focus of 'Ode', dated 4 July 1918, invites the notion that Eliot may have done so. It may even mark the beginning of a project whose aim was precisely to 'escape history'.

The looming alliance of the United States and Britain certainly overshadows the drawn-out dance of that marriage to some degree. In fact, the surrounding discourse upon which the Archbishop of York freely draws, suggests a general broadening of focus in which any Haigh-Wood/Eliot relationship could hardly avoid the embrace of the Anglo-American union whose implications it symbolizes. 'History is making plain the truth that these two English-speaking peoples have a common destiny in which the welfare of the world is involved', the Archbishop declared. Indeed, as he continues, that destiny starts to take on the clearest of matrimonial dimensions:

> Those whom God has manifestly joined together by a community of tradition and of spirit must never be put asunder. From their indissoluble union may a new hope for the peace and freedom of the world be born.[55]

In the light of the carnage of Flanders and elsewhere (the major German breakthrough of the *Kaiserschlacht* had taken place in France only the preceding March), the Archbishop's marriage metaphor does more than set 'Ode's' references to blood on the marriage bed in a new and terrible perspective. Its ironic and unwitting reversal of a 400-year-old metaphor in which the Old World fertilized the New would hardly have escaped Eliot. But its bland announcement to a culturally violated Britain of the birth of a new hope for peace and freedom perhaps also suggests why a deflowering Coriolanus might eventually turn from such pious vapourings in disgust.

It is a disgust which fully permeates 'Ode' and perhaps finally renders it incoherent. Eliot was certainly unhappy with the result. He suppressed the poem almost immediately on publication, and was extremely anxious that his mother should not see it. He even considered cutting the relevant page out of the copy of *Ara Vos Prec* which he sent to her.[56] When, a few months after the occasion the poem commemorates, Woodrow Wilson became the first American President to visit Britain and drove in triumph through the streets of London, Eliot seems almost to go out of his way to describe the spectacle to his mother in terms that he no doubt felt would be more in accord with that lady's sensibilities:

> There was a huge crowd, and the streets were all hung with American flags. It was really an extraordinary and inspiring occasion. I do not believe that people in America realise how much Wilson's policy has done to inspire respect for America abroad. I think that *all* the nations, allied, hostile, and neutral, *trust* us as they trust no other. . . . America certainly has a more disinterested record of foreign policy (at least from the time of John Hay) than any other country.

The same overt enthusiasm about the impact of America on Europe is reflected in Vivien's response to the same occasion in a letter to Charlotte C. Eliot:

> Tom and I went early and stood in the best place we could find, for over 2 hours. Even then we had quite 30 *rows* of people deep in front of us – and I should have seen nothing at all if Tom had not lifted me up just as they passed. It was a most moving and wonderful sight to see him sitting next the King, and having such a glorious welcome.[57]

But perhaps this was for public consumption. For by the time something like this event had been crystallized into verse, other dimensions of the situation were being signalled by the savage irony of the title Eliot gave to his later piece, 'Triumphal March':

> Stone, bronze, stone, steel, stone, oakleaves, horses' heels
> Over the paving.
> And the flags. And the trumpets. And so many eagles.
> How many? Count them. And such a press of people.

We hardly knew ourselves that day, or knew the City.
This is the way to the temple, and we so many crowding the way.
So many waiting, how many waiting? what did it matter, on
such a day?
Are they coming? No, not yet. You can see some eagles. And
hear the trumpets.
Here they come. Is he coming?
The natural wakeful life of our Ego is a perceiving.
We can wait with our stools and our sausages

Here American eagles merge with Roman ones as the poem's involvement with Wilson's triumphal entry into London is cemented by an
ironic but apparently accurate citing of details of the armaments
surrendered by the Germans to the Allies after the Treaty of Versailles,
taken almost verbatim from Ludendorff's *The Coming War* (1931).[58]

5,800,000 rifles and carbines,
102,000 machine guns,
28,000 trench mortars
53,000 field and heavy guns . . . [etc.]

Nevertheless, as with 'Ode', the attempt to process large political
issues by means of indirect ironic confrontation through poetry
seems to have struck Eliot as a failure. After its publication, together
with the related 'Difficulties of a Statesman' in 1931–2, both pieces
were consigned to the category of 'Unfinished Poems'. But it is not
without significance that the title Eliot gave to the sequence was
Coriolan.

The impulses leading to that choice of topic are obviously complex
and perhaps they reach back to the earliest days of Eliot's arrival in
Britain and his developing concept of his function here. Of course, on
a personal level, the figure of Coriolanus offered an overt model for
a crucial relationship within his own family. Coriolanus and Eliot
could each be said to have done what he did 'to please his mother
and be partly proud'. Perhaps Coriolanus's ultimate threat to ravish
even his 'mother city' Rome, to 'treade' on his 'Mother's womb/That
brought thee to this world' suggests a subtler urgency, matching
Eliot's drive towards literary success in what was then the supreme
foreign 'motherland' of his language's culture. But there are areas of
broader significance. By now, Vivien's perceptive British eye notes a
new emphasis:

We all follow American politics now, although before the war I
suppose no ordinary English person knew anything about them.[59]

Eliot took a darker view. He later refers to Wilson's collapse 'before European diplomacy' at the Peace Conference, and of his 'grave mistake in coming to Europe'.[60] In a sense, it confirmed his own. Both perhaps seemed Coriolanus-like acts of forced entry into a citadel followed by a shaming intimacy with despised allies to the extent that Caius Martius's experiences as 'penetrator' of walled cities such as Corioles, Antium, even Rome, seem appropriate to aspects of each enterprise.[61] Edward Mandell House, Wilson's adviser, claimed that the President's 'supreme mistake' lay in his decision to attend the Peace Conference at Versailles in person.

He was the God in the Mountain and his decisions regarding international matters were practically final. When he came to Europe and sat in conference with the Prime Ministers and representatives of other states, he gradually lost his place as first citizen of the world.[62]

Writing to his brother in 1919, Eliot complains of the belittling differences that characterize his own exposure to London/Volscian cultural life:

Don't think that I find it easy to live over here. It's damned hard work to live with a foreign nation and cope with them – one is always coming up against differences of feeling that make one feel humiliated and lonely. One remains always a foreigner – only the lower classes can assimilate.[63]

Yeats's observations on the portrait of Wilson quoted above, presenting him as the alienated non-European intellectual, his mind separated from his body by a yawning dissociation of sensibilities, would undoubtedly have struck a chord in Eliot. Wilson's final, fatal breakdown in 1919 perhaps suggests him as the 'broken Coriolanus' of *The Waste Land*. In any event, the poet who mourned the decline of lower-class English culture in the music hall could not but have been sensitive to the destructive aspects of the American cultural penetration of Europe which were to some degree responsible for it, and in which American music and dancing were potent weapons. The disgust at the self-perpetrated blood on the bridal sheets offered in 'Ode' suggests one metaphor for the process, but there were others no less appropriate. As he confided to his mother in 1920, 'getting recognised in English letters is like breaking open a safe – for an American'. And later the same year he confessed to Scofield Thayer that 'London is a tough nut to crack'.[64]

However, a Coriolanus-like arrogance sustains him. Both are

authors. Coriolanus, notoriously, is 'author of himself'. And Eliot, in so far as he offered to rewrite British literary traditions in order to place himself as their latest successor, had a broadly similar aim. As he put it to Maxwell Bodenheim, in haughty terms that Coriolanus himself might have employed,

> I have, moreover, a certain persistent curiosity about the English and a desire to see whether they can ever be roused to anything like intellectual activity . . . Once there was a civilisation here, I believe, that's a curious and exciting point. This is not conceit, merely a kind of pugnacity.[65]

Linked, in that pugnacious, penetrative adventure, with Shakespeare's protagonist, perhaps Eliot felt himself implicated in an American tragedy whose outlines *Coriolanus* surely hints at. Certainly, the final stanza of 'Ode', with its reference to the departure of Andromeda's monster/lover, hints at the sort of baffled and hurt withdrawal that has long been part of the American experience of Europe.[66] Witnessing it at various levels from Woodrow Wilson to Ezra Pound ('I know absolutely nothing to England's credit . . . No Englishman's word is worth a damn', wrote Pound),[67] and perhaps even sensing its stirrings in his own relationship with Vivien, Eliot cast the experience in terms that echo not only Macbeth's observation on the consequences to himself of the murder of his king, ('The deep damnation of his taking off') but also Coriolanus's angry commitment to self-exile

> I go alone,
> Like to a lonely dragon that his fen
> Makes fear'd and talk'd of more than seen
> (IV, i, 29–31)

The figures of Wilson, Coriolanus and Eliot himself seem almost to merge here, in the voice of a betrayer of his people who finally finds himself betrayed.

The Original Dixieland One-Step

Another view of history perhaps offered redemption, and by the time of the Second World War, Eliot was able to see his own role in respect of British culture quite differently. In fact, by 1940, and with the publication of 'East Coker', his had become a distinctive English voice. It was more than a matter of phonetics, although the last traces of what he liked to call the 'nigger drawl' of Missouri, to say nothing of his New England mannerisms, had long since been smoothed away. Eliot's was now the voice of an Englishness distilled by the threat of extinction.

It was a time of sweeping military defeats in Europe and increasing British isolation, climaxing in the débâcle of Dunkirk. With her back to the wall, Chamberlain deposed, Churchill installed, Britain faced invasion and wholesale collapse. It was left to no less a proponent of the quintessential nature of Englishness than F. R. Leavis to signal Eliot's position. He was, said the voice of Cambridge in a letter to the *Times Literary Supplement* complaining about its review of 'East Coker', 'the greatest living English poet'. He even asked, in an astonishing compounding of the irony, 'What other poet have we now that Yeats is gone?'[68] Eliot had evidently come a long way from St Louis.

'East Coker' appeared in the Easter 1940 issue of the *New English Weekly* and made an immediate impact. Faber & Faber published it as a pamphlet in September of that year and it sold nearly twelve thousand copies. The poem's overall manner seems cautious, defensive, and its focus, appropriately, is on continuity, tradition, Englishness. Its setting is crucial to its strategy. East Coker was the home of Andrew Eliot, Eliot's forebear, who had left the village for America two hundred years previously. A key passage, apparently in the poet's own voice, takes up most of these concerns:

> In my beginning is my end. Now the light falls
> Across the open field, leaving the deep lane
> Shuttered with branches, dark in the afternoon,
> Where you lean against a bank while a van passes,
> And the deep lane insists on the direction
> Into the village, in the electric heat
> Hypnotised. In a warm haze the sultry light
> Is absorbed, not refracted, by grey stone.
> The dahlias sleep in the empty silence.
> Wait for the early owl.
>
>   In that open field
> If you do not come too close, if you do not come too close,
> On a summer midnight, you can hear the music
> Of the weak pipe and the little drum
> And see them dancing around the bonfire
> The association of man and woman
> In daunsinge, signifying matrimonie—
> A dignified and commodious sacrament.

Two and two, necessarye coniunction,
Holding eche other by the hand or the arm
Whiche betokeneth concorde. Round and round the fire
Leaping through the flames, or joined in circles,
Rustically solemn or in rustic laughter
Lifting heavy feet in clumsy shoes,
Earth feet, loam feet, lifted in country mirth
Mirth of those long since under earth
Nourishing the corn. Keeping time,
Keeping the rhythm in their dancing
As in their living in the living seasons
The time of the seasons and the constellations
The time of milking and the time of harvest
The time of the coupling of man and woman
And that of beasts. Feet rising and falling.
Eating and drinking. Dung and death.

(ll. 14–46)

Some of the initial themes of this essay begin to resurface here. The poet as 'spy' makes an obvious appearance, creeping into East Coker, leaning into a bank as a van passes, observing the natives closely whilst maintaining an appropriately alienated and watchful distance, careful to advise that 'you do not come too close', almost as if he were indeed the agent of a foreign power. He is even dark-skinned, with an odd way of speaking, a man of superior ability, who is frequently publishing. Spy Nozy, reincarnated here in the Eliot who once wrote of the poet's capacity to amalgamate the experiences of falling in love, the smell of cooking and reading Spinoza, can have had few better representatives in our century, though it is not recorded that the villagers of East Coker reported him to the police.[69]

One of the most startling devices is, of course, Eliot's insertion into the poem of a passage concerning dancing from his forebear Sir Thomas Elyot's work *The Boke Named The Governour*;

The association of man and woman
In daunsinge, signifying matrimonie—
A dignified and commodious sacrament.
Two and two, necessarye coniunction,
Holding eche other by the hand or the arm
Whiche betokeneth concorde.

(ll. 28–33)

This aims to enact one of the central points of the poem, that we can make genuine and fruitful contact with the past, and even address and listen to it directly. Indeed, the historical difference between Eliot and Elyot seems to dissolve before our eyes as the hand of the sixteenth-century writer contributes lines to a twentieth-century poem. History is gently drained away in this courtly dance. So much for the Archbishop of York's First World War claim that 'we cannot escape history'. The wished-for 'marriage' between the two English-speaking cultures proposed in 1918 seems readily consummated here, in this celebration of 'matrimonie' in 1940. And there is no blood on the sheets, despite the fact that a war once again lends urgency to the project.

Unfortunately, Eliot's impersonation of his ancestor fails to suppress history entirely. In fact, decades later, he is taken to task by F. R. Leavis precisely because of his failure to make sympathetic contact with the feudal culture whose less artful gyrations he describes here as

> Rustically solemn or in rustic laughter
> Lifting heavy feet in clumsy shoes,
> Earth feet, loam feet, lifted in country mirth
> (ll. 35–7)

Leavis argues that the unthinking 'reductive effect' of this account of clod-hopping country dancing turns into mere 'yokels' those whose 'organic culture' had 'created the English language that made Shakespeare possible'. In fact, he seems to say that it is Eliot's experience as an American that makes him unable to give that peasant culture the serious status it warrants: 'Whatever he might assent to formally, in a notional way, he couldn't in his imaginative, his vital thinking, conceive of a sophisticated art that grows out of a total organic culture.'[70] Certainly, Eliot's rendition of that feudal dance,

> Feet rising and falling.
> Eating and drinking. Dung and death.
> (ll. 45–6)

seems to embody a sense of its ultimate futility. Perhaps the trans-atlantic 'feudal/futile' elision is slyly and metaphorically at work, despite what must have been strenuous efforts on Eliot's part to reduce its phonetic presence in his own speech. Perhaps to see the 'feudal' as 'futile' is to be essentially American. And perhaps that requires him, finally, to remain a foxtrotting Eliot, however strong the desire to merge with a 'daunsinge' Elyot. In other words, historical difference, far from dissolving, remains sufficiently concrete to ensure that Eliot – like the rest of us – can only ever spy upon, and can never become one with, his forebears.

The ultimate function of the Elyot passage in Eliot's poem confirms that situation. In a highly self-conscious text, full of self-reference,

> That was a way of putting it—not very satisfactory:
> A periphrastic study in a worn-out poetical fashion,
> Leaving one still with the intolerable wrestle
> With words and meanings.
>
> (ll. 68–71)

the passage from *The Boke Named The Governour* takes on a kind of emblematic role as its lively sense of bodily movement is first ingested and then digested by the poem's account of a final engorging reality of dung and death. If, in the process, the text manages non-discursively to 'dance' with the Elyot passage, in a necessary conjunction betokening concord between the centuries, the mode in which it does so could be said none the less to be the cocooning, domesticating modern one promulgated most famously by Victor Silvester: slow, slow, quick quick, slow. As Silvester tamed American dancing to suit British manners, so a former American dancer now tailors his adopted culture's past to suit the exigencies of the present. Sir Thomas Elyot's 'quick' here finds itself caged and tranquillized by T. S. Eliot's surrounding, restraining 'slow'.

That, of course, is how it strikes a British contemporary. But there can be no doubt that the *Four Quartets*, offering as they do an extended contemplation of time, see what is perhaps a different role for their author. The submerged metaphor which energizes the contemplation has links with dancing as fundamental as those it has with music; with the paradox that the time-bound movement of dance nevertheless depends upon and reveals a timeless 'still point' around which the dance is structured. In 'Burnt Norton', for example, the case is firmly put that 'Except for the point, the still point,/There would be no dance, and there is only the dance' (ll. 66–7) and that 'at the still point, there the dance is' (l. 63).

Throughout the *Quartets* the horror of being imprisoned 'in time' frequently surfaces. Mere existence threatens, it seems, its own ineluctably 'strict tempo' binding humans and animals alike:

> Keeping time,
> Keeping the rhythm in their dancing
> As in their living in the living seasons
> The time of the seasons and the constellations
> The time of milking and the time of harvest
> The time of the coupling of man and woman
> And that of beasts.
>
> ('East Coker', ll. 39–45)

And European history, that no less 'strict tempo' commitment to the march of time, no doubt imposes its burdens on other cultures. There is an obvious sense in which the entire American project, like all revolutionary endeavours, has been an attempt to 'escape history' of that sort and Eliot's reiterated effort to break out of the movement of time, and into the stillness which lies beyond, is perhaps his most American characteristic.

'Tradition' was always one instrument for doing so, a means of proclaiming a kind of retrievable, instantaneous linking across the years which denied the separating claims of time. Another way seemed to lie through dance. For Eliot, dancing seems almost to offer a kind of immersion in a preparatory burning purgatory from which only stillness brings relief, and this metaphor runs throughout his verse, from the unpublished 'The Burnt Dancer', through 'The Death of Saint Narcissus',

> So he became a dancer to God.
> Because his flesh was in love with the burning arrows
> He danced on the hot sand
> Until the arrows came.

until it surfaces in works such as 'Little Gidding' in 1942 which speaks of

> that refining fire
> Where you must move in measure, like a dancer.[71]
>
> (ll. 145–6)

The aim of such movement is to dance beyond the restraining 'measure', the strict tempo, in order to reach the freedom of stillness. That freedom, that immobility, constitutes of course the point at which the dancer's troublesome personality finally ebbs away and, as Yeats had it, becomes indistinguishable from the dance itself. Eliot gestures towards this sort of freedom when he writes of

> music heard so deeply
> That it is not heard at all, but you are the music
> While the music lasts.
>> ('The Dry Salvages', ll. 210–12)

In historical terms, the project involves breaking through the 'dance' of the years, and finding the unmoving permanence which lies at its heart: or, as Eliot put it in 'Triumphal March', finding 'the still point of the turning world'. That poem's presentation of President Wilson as a Coriolanus spurned by an ungrateful mob attempts exactly that feat: it aims to break through immediacy (the year 1918, the Treaty of Versailles) to touch the permanent (the story of Coriolanus and of Rome) beyond. The synchronic presentation of the crass and transient present (the narrow early life of the uncomprehending telephone operator Arthur Edward Cyril Parker) and the permanently transcendent (Christ's entry into Jerusalem, Coriolanus's into Rome) is presumably a planned feature of the failed whole.

This is as much as to say that, despite his intense and ultimately corrupting Anglophilia, Eliot remained a modern American poet to the last. His Modernism, as was argued above, betrays itself in the anti-historical stance he never finally abandoned. Paul de Man has made the point that 'modernity' in all its forms manifests a latent animus against history, against the pastness of a past which is yet able to exert pressure on the present. Fundamentally, Modernism embodies a 'desire to wipe out whatever came earlier' in pursuit of 'a radically new departure, a point that could be a true present'. Nietzsche's proposal that the fruitfulness of that present rests on and demands a wilful amnesia strikes de Man as a crucial aspect of Modernism, for 'Nietzsche's ruthless forgetting, the blindness with which he throws himself into action lightened of all previous experience, captures the authentic spirit of modernity.' The result, de Man concludes, is that 'modernity and history are diametrically opposed to each other'.[72] Thus, Eliot characteristically excises the past, folding it, in 'Triumphal March' as elsewhere, into the present, always claiming that it lacks any material and defining difference:

> So, while the light fails
> On a winter's afternoon, in a secluded chapel
> History is now and England.
>> ('Little Gidding', ll. 135–7)

Meanwhile, the England he wished to preserve, the England that 'East Coker' spies upon, only finally made sense for him in American terms, as a part of Europe. As Peter Ackroyd suggests, he sought to become, like Henry James, 'a European . . . in a way that no person born in Europe could be'.[73] It might even be said that he promoted an extension of what, since 1945, has been American foreign policy in regard to Britain and Europe: the Common Market.

This policy sees Europe as one place, a single unified entity (somehow until recently excluding countries behind the 'Iron Curtain'). Leavis's peculiar assessment of Eliot focuses on and exemplifies the contradiction involved. For Leavis, Eliot may on the one hand be the greatest living English poet, but on the other hand he lacks native Englishness. It is of course arguable that the latter is a prerequisite of the former. Natives rarely make good nationals.

For British culture, a related paradox lies at the heart of the 'special relationship' so frequently proposed with the United States, a society whose language is English, but whose culture is not. History now mocks at the suggestion, implicit in the pronouncements of 1917, that a British 'slow' might be able to contain and direct an American 'quick'. America now makes Europe (and Britain) its frontier and even, in some respects, its front line. Eliot, American agent that he always was, perhaps also served the same end. Elsewhere in the *Four Quartets*, in 'Burnt Norton' for example (the poem that precedes 'East Coker'), he characteristically foregrounds and privileges a 'quickness', a living 'now', at the expense of the slow 'waste sad time' of history:

> the hidden laughter
> Of children in the foliage
> Quick now, here, now, always—
> Ridiculous the waste sad time
> Stretching before and after.
> ('Burnt Norton', ll. 71–5)

But that immediacy, the asserted unity and oneness, that American 'Quick now, here, now, always' in whose light the time 'Stretching before and after' seems merely ridiculous, requires and depends upon an occlusion of the past which is part and parcel of a deconstruction of the opposition between the temporal and the eternal in terms of that between Dance and Stillness or Slowness and Quickness. Repeated in the final lines of 'Little Gidding', the last of the *Quartets*,

> Quick now, here, now, always—
> A condition of complete simplicity
> (Costing not less than everything)

it reveals itself as an attempt to ditch history, to abandon 'everything' in the name of that timeless simplicity which has always been attractive to the kind of American discourse committed to the construction of a single, transcendent, coherent vision.

We can label this legacy of the New World to the Old the 'Original Dixieland One-Step': a rendition, in dance, of a thesis concerning singularity, oneness, unity, which generates (via Virgil's *Moretum*) the motto of the United States of America itself, and is proclaimed on the back of every dollar bill: *E Pluribus Unum*. The abolition of difference proposed here means that the past can have no claim on the present. *Hamlet*, by its light, remains inexplicable, unrecuperable, intractable. *Coriolanus*, on the other hand, speaks with mastery of our permanent concerns. What confronts us in such a judgement is nothing less than a history-denying American cakewalk to which Europe – despite the best efforts of Victor Silvester and his 'English style' – now finds itself required to move. Perhaps the proud Coriolanus has at last achieved his ambition in banishing us. Is it just a fantasy that Mr Walsh, government agent, scratching his rather prominent nose, would probably report nothing wrong with that?

6   Lear's Maps

Meantime

'Meantime', says the King, rising to his feet and glowering at his audience, 'we shall express our darker purpose.'

Like King Lear's, my own – slightly less dark – purpose involves a redrawing and a reshaping of what may to some seem familiar ground. So the monarch's next lines are not inappropriate to my design. I am proposing to draw a map, or a series of maps, of recent developments in Shakespearean criticism in Britain. And I can begin with *King Lear*, and with those very lines, because in a crucial sense they focus precisely on Britain itself:

> Give me the map there. Know that we have divided
> In three our kingdom
>
>   (I, i, 38–41)

If we insert this passage into the context of its own material history at the beginning of the seventeenth century, we can hardly fail to notice what might be called its *emblematic* force. The threatening words 'Give me the map there', and the consequent unfurling of a programme of brutal partition, pitch the play into the middle of a complex discursive arena in which the spectre of political and social disintegration confronts and interrogates King James's efforts to present the throne as the source and guarantee of social coherence.

To make this sort of manoeuvre, tucking the work back into its own time, is to invoke a kind of historicism. And whilst the release of the lines' emblematic dimension may lend them a surprising energy, the gambit's slightly self-conscious air perhaps proves disconcerting. It derives from the fact that, more than any other, a recourse to and engagement with history can be said to be the characteristic gesture of recent British and American Shakespearean criticism.

The use of history involved, however, is of a particular order. It differs radically from another sort still dominant on both sides of the Atlantic, which tends to focus on historical material as if it formed a 'background' against which literary texts might profitably be placed before being read. Whilst that procedure seems innocuous enough, a series of assumptions can be seen to fuel it and finally to shape its conclusions. Chief amongst them is a notion of the literary text as a privileged vehicle of communication, perhaps functioning most fruitfully when located in some kind of historical context, but in the end finally independent of it. A covert distinction between text and context, foreground and background, evidently operates here on behalf of some further and quite major presuppositions. One of them involves a simple projection of the values of our own near-universal literacy onto the past. Another reflects an undeclared investment in a view of history warped by its primary commitment to the academic study of literature.

One of the main concerns of what has come to be known as the New Historicism will be to renegotiate that distinction between foreground and background: to relocate and then re-read literary texts in quite a different relation to the other material signifying practices of a culture. As its name suggests, New Historicism's own history also involves a programme of radical readjustment. On the one hand it represents a reaction against a de-historicized idealism, in which an apparently free-floating and autonomous body of writing called 'literature' serves as the repository of the universal values of a supposedly permanent 'human nature'. On the other, it constitutes a rejection of the presuppositions of a 'history of ideas', which tends to regard literature as a static mirror of its time. Such a historicism's 'newness' lies precisely in its determination to reposition 'literature' altogether, to perceive literary texts as active constituent *elements* of their time, participants in, not mirrors of it; respondent to and involved with numerous other enterprises, such as the law, marriage, religion, government, all engaged in the production of 'texts' and the cultural meanings that finally constitute a way of life. And it will see these, and particularly the relations of power which operate between them, as equally determining features in respect of particular societies and their culture.

The whole project clearly owes something to the work of Foucault, and it finally calls, as Leonard Tennenhouse has argued, for a major 'unthinking' of our own appropriating, segregating procedures, particularly those by which we 'enclose Renaissance culture within our own discourse and thus make it speak our notion of sexuality, the family, and the individual.'[1] Shakespeare's plays, such an 'unthinking' suggests, function as part of a quite different discursive order whose contours, boundaries and dispositions of experience are hardly likely to match those we nowadays take for granted. They spring from and engage with a world quite distinct from our own: one in which, for instance, as Tennenhouse demonstrates, literary and political discourses have yet to be differentiated. Like other contemporaneous texts (the distinctions between them often invented by ourselves), Shakespeare's plays participate in their society in terms of their capacity to make sense in and of and for it. They thus take their place in an extensive symbolic field which must also include royal proclamations, parliamentary debates, architecture, music, song, letters and travellers' reports as aspects of a number of different rhetorical or 'textual' strategies available and consistently utilized for the production of meaning. Clearly, such a symbolic field also includes the potent texts that we call maps.

Old times

On this basis, then, it is precisely at the moment when Lear calls for the map that the play begins to engage with issues of large cultural concern and starts to contribute to their discussion. Two matters seem particularly important as a result.

First, the map itself – a supposedly definitive 'text' in respect of the kingdom it offers to determine – hints at a reductive quality in Lear's purpose that a largely pre-literate audience would have surely recognized and responded to. Maps may purport to be objective, accurate, impartial in character but, as our own century knows to its cost, they inevitably turn out to be extensions and implementations of specific political and moral positions. Maps, in short, are never innocent. They can also, as here, operate to reduce an imprecisely defined but none the less emotionally charged, numinous and multi-level sense of 'nationhood' to the merely literal, physical, one-dimensional standing of a piece of paper. The sense of maps as insuperably divisive and reductive, the means whereby men or women illicitly intervene in and degrade a divinely sanctioned order of being, is emblematically depicted, for example, in Shakespeare's *1 Henry IV*, in the notable scene in which the rebels pore over their charts to divide their prospective but ill-gotten gains (III, i, 69ff.).

Second, the fact that it is Lear who calls for the map generates a crucial oxymoron whose tragic implications become fundamental to the play's agenda: the King, the virtual fount of social, political and spiritual unity here reveals himself to be the actual cause of cataclysmic, boundary-drawing division.

We can be quite specific about the implications of the latter point. The accession of the King of Scotland to the throne of England in 1603 threatened a revolutionary change in British politics. James's propaganda machine dealt with this by resuscitating the story of Merlin's prophecy, whereby a second Brutus would return in triumph to the British New Troy established by his predecessor. The first Trojan Brutus had founded Troynovant (i.e. London) on the banks of the Thames, but had then proceeded disastrously to divide his kingdom between his three sons, thus producing Wales, England and Scotland. The second Brutus would re-unite the realm, which would then be named, in his honour, Great Britain.

Official history presents James precisely in this reconstructive mode. His accession in 1603 is said to have preserved Britain from foreign invasion and civil war. The timely discovery – or invention – of the Gunpowder Plot on 5 November 1605 confirmed his role as national saviour. The union of the two crowns by Act of Parliament in 1608 gave it final sanction. And these events were then processed as 'miraculous' by a discourse which made use of prophecies, legends and portents to weave what Glynne Wickham has called the 'rhetoric and literature of a new messianic vision' with James and his family at its centre.[2]

Indeed, James made no bones about that. He presented himself not only as the second Brutus, and not only as the saviour, but as the 'father' of his country (*parens patriae*), with appropriate extensions of the metaphor to yield astonishing proclamations such as 'I am the Husbande and all the whole Isle is my lawful wife: I am the Head, and it is my Body; I am the Shepherd and it is my flocke'. On this basis, he proceeded to adopt as his personal motto the designation *Beati Pacifici*, and it is from this moment that the words 'Great Britain' first become current as a way of talking about – indeed of mapping – the terrain involved.

King Lear, to say nothing of *Macbeth*, is surely part of this discourse and speaks from inside and in harmony with it. At this level, the material impact of the map placed before Lear – a whole pre-literate, spiritually-conceived culture shockingly reduced to and treated as a physical diagram – must be considerable, and its implications must constitute credible aspects of the play's complex project. In short, Lear's division of the kingdom emerges as far more than the whimsical folly of an old man. It offers to tease out for its audience the ramifications of a political and social disaster whose proportions foreshadow and comment on contemporary events, or pseudo-events, such as the Gunpowder Plot. As a result, it takes its place as part of a symbolic field extending beyond the theatre to the concerns of the culture at large, and the point would readily be made by some divisive gesture in respect of the physical map itself. It is not without significance that Goneril's husband is called Albany (the old name for Scotland) and that Regan's husband is called Cornwall (the old name for Wales and the west of England). These portions might even be literally torn from Lear's map and handed to their recipients as they speak, leaving Cordelia's 'third more opulent than your sisters' raggedly but evidently and, to a London audience, appropriately signalled as England.

New times

Efforts to distinguish between New Historicism, by and large a phenomenon of the American academy, and Cultural Materialism, its supposed British counterpart, have to contend with the fact that the two projects appear to occupy quite a lot of common ground. Hugh Grady sees them both as 'postmodernisms', dealing in a 'decentred' notion of art and speaking to and on behalf of a fragmented subject who creates and perceives it.[3] In addition to the features already mentioned, both seem committed to two fundamental projects: first, the abandonment of 'organic unity' as the appropriate model of a culture's essential or achievable condition, as well as the chief aesthetic value to which the practice of art within it should aspire, and second, the rejection or deconstruction of those binary oppositions which currently determine our own world-view and that of past cultures.

In the place of 'organic unity', both New Historicism and Cultural Materialism offer a view of cultures as inherently disunified, hegemonic structures, characteristically held together at any specific time by tensions between competing interests and different practices. Never static or finished, always in process, such arrangements seem permanently to teeter on the edge of disintegration.

Binary oppositions, of course, constitute the crucial grounding of the business of cultural meaning and ultimately of identity itself: we are what we oppose. So, a project which undertakes to lay bare (in order to make open to change) the principles of that identity's construction will require fundamental conceptual polarities, such as 'high culture' and 'popular culture', masculinity and femininity, 'moral' and 'immoral' to be challenged and the relationship of their component parts to be reassessed, if not unpicked. This kind of deconstructive analysis and its major conclusion – that such funda-mental oppositions are the temporary products of history, politics, or way of life rather than permanent features of nature – gives a voice to those elements of the society which at a given moment find them-selves the disfavoured partners in their respective oppositions: the ones condemned, that is, to be marginalized, displaced, sub-ordinated, demonized, repressed or criminalized.

Both New Historicism and Cultural Materialism tend to present these neglected, discounted aspects of society as, in the last analysis, truly definitive of its nature. As Grady points out, the result is an emphatic redrawing of what used to be termed the 'Elizabethan World Picture'. This ceases to be the organic, unified Golden Age described by E. M. W. Tillyard and instead appears as an age of cruelty, imprisonment, torture; given, like our own, to complex programmes of marginalization, dehumanization and alienation.[4] We are, in this sense, what we silence. But in the analyses of New Historicism and Cultural Materialism, the silenced speak.

None the less, crucial differences of emphasis remain. It has become commonplace to say that in some New Historicist studies, for example, a somewhat positivist or 'objective' recuperation and representation of the past seems at times to be on offer. As a result, the Elizabethan theatre appears virtually to function as an instrument of direct political containment, sanctioned for that purpose by a knowing establishment. It is as if each group of plays spoke with a single voice, and to a single, albeit complex and many-layered brief.

Fruitful, unlooked-for contradiction naturally becomes an early casualty in such a process. The text begins to seem smoothly conducive to whatever the creature 'Shakespeare' thinks and believes, with small allowance made for its own textuality, its own cross-grained recalcitrance, its refusal to say one thing and one thing only, its function, then as much as now, as arena or battleground. The political state it engages with seems correspondingly static, drained of a potential for radical resistance and sleekly recuperative of the dissent which we now know lay in wait.[5]

Cultural Materialism, on the other hand, seems eager (over-eager, some opponents would have it) to seek out the complexities of refusal and rejection embedded in early modern texts and anxious to respond sympathetically to the smallest signs of resist-ance wherever these may be found. It pursues these quarries, friend and foe seem to agree, with a vigour perhaps born of the more harshly divisive tenor of British life. In general terms, its first principles are certainly rooted in the British commitment and orientation of the work of Raymond Williams. Terry Eagleton has made the point that the essence of Williams's position lies in his insistence that all aspects of culture are actually and materially present in the world we inhabit; none enjoys 'ideal' or 'immaterial' status.[6] Culture abides in day-to-day practice: it does not and cannot transcend material economic social and political conditions, and it is vested, not in particular enterprises within a way of life, but in the whole range of activities that make up the way of life itself. 'Culture' thus involves the entire spectrum of whatever people get up to in concrete terms in the material world.

Like New Historicism, Cultural Materialism declines to privilege literature, or to accord writing any 'transcendent' dimension or quality. It places those activities firmly in the context of the general social process, and thus on a par with the activities of subordinate or marginalized groups. In other words, it takes 'high culture' to be, as Jonathan Dollimore and Alan Sinfield have described it, just 'one set of signifying practices among others'.[7] Committed, by that notion of 'practice', to the idea that we are involved in the continuous 'making' rather than the discovery of cultural meanings, to what I have described as the business of 'meaning by', such a materialism ultimately perceives culture as volatile, undecided, never complete or 'finished', but always in process; always riven, for example, by tensions between at least three modes of historical development which exist concurrently, and which Williams categorizes as the Emergent, the Dominant, and the Residual.[8]

The central distinction between New Historicism and Cultural Materialism resides in the view each takes of the Elizabethan project of social and political containment, and the role played in it by the drama and the public theatres. As Dollimore formulates the issue, 'did [Shakespeare's] plays reinforce the dominant order, or do they interrogate it to the point of subversion? According to a rough and ready division, new historicists have inclined to the first view, cultural materialists to the second'.[9] Elsewhere, he comments that 'the two movements have differed over just this: it is new historicism which has been accused of finding too much containment, while cultural materialism has been accused of finding too much sub-version'.[10]

However this difference may or may not ultimately be resolved, the fundamental contribution of both Cultural Materialism and New Historicism clearly lies in the perception that whether it is being reinforced or interrogated, any power that shows itself to be susceptible to either operation can never, by that fact, have been totally embracing or entirely dominant. Never a seamless garment, power can only partly cover the body politic. Resistance to it is therefore always theoretically and usually practically possible, even inevitable, and indeed is obviously presupposed by the very existence of strategies of containment. To a considerable extent, power's specific nature will reveal itself in the shape such strategies take.[11]

A drama's interrogation of power will, in turn, require it both to draw upon and adjust its own resources to match whatever forms of subjection it encounters.[12] To take just one example; as part of its everyday operations, the Elizabethan theatre was forced to confront the sumptuary laws of a society which permitted certain modes of dress and proscribed others in order to signify specific rankings amongst its citizens. The theatre's own inherited practice of gender cross-dressing, and indeed the broad nature of its art at large, which required commoners to dress as nobility, even royalty, was bound systematically to conflict with those modes of enforcing gender and class distinctions, bringing them into question and, ultimately, to the point of crisis. It thus found itself inescapably engaged with political domination in that particular material form, and as a result could hardly avoid questioning its authority. For whatever overt statements a play may make, its performance on the Elizabethan stage tacitly and simultaneously also proposes that it is custom, or culture, rather than God, or nature, that separates one class from another, and even male from female. In the early modern period, such ideas were explosive, and an adversarial literary criticism will obviously seek to point this out. In the words of Frank Lentricchia, 'Ruling culture does not define the whole of culture, though it tries to, and it is the task of the oppositional critic to re-read culture so as to amplify and strategically position the marginalised voices of the ruled, exploited, oppressed and excluded.'[13]

Of course, Cultural Materialism also recognizes that power can seek to generate subversion for its own ends, in order to make its own task of containment easier. A faked Gunpowder Plot, easily put down, would perhaps have had even greater propaganda value than a genuine one: the systematic stimulation of moral panic to serve an establishment's own ends is an ancient stratagem of rule. However, once installed, a mode of subversion remains willy-nilly available for appropriation, and becomes part of the complex of contending forces which governments must learn to orchestrate. For political and social power is rarely monolithic and never total. Material 'rule' is far more likely to consist of a balance shakily maintained between different, competing elements within the sort of uneasy stand-off that finally characterizes a containing way of life.

A historicist criticism, capable of recognizing the complexities of this kind of permanent contestation of meaning both in the past and in the present, cannot and does not, unlike traditional criticism, pretend to be politically neutral. For it 'knows that no cultural practice is ever without political significance' and it recognizes that that principle applies to itself.[14] Its project will thus be deliberately interventionist in the name of the here and now. Committed both to the study of 'the implication of literary texts in history' and to 'the transformation of a social order which exploits people on grounds of race, gender and class', it is thereby committed to seeing history as an arena, a site of struggle where, in the name of this commitment, battle must be joined.[15] And it sees, to mix the metaphor, the past as the jewel in the crown of the present.

As part of its concern with the present, such a historicism will finally set out to situate the text within the cultural field determined by our own array of signifying practices, one of the most potent of these being a system of education which seeks to process it on behalf of specific political positions and ambitions. This area is of course also perceived as contestable, open to argument. And readings of the text won as a result of locating it in its 'original' context become powerful weapons in the contest for its standing in ours. The past, not merely a jewel, functions also as a strategically placed ballistic missile, trained on the present.

Wartime

That bellicose image aptly prompts a change of focus, bringing into view a production of *King Lear* which took place some three hundred years after the performance described above. I refer to the famous version of the play, directed by Harley Granville-Barker, and starring John Gielgud, which ran at the Old Vic Theatre in London from 15 April to 25 May in the year 1940.

It has already been pointed out that Granville-Barker was well known for his 'innovations' in Shakespearean production. In effect, these were stratagems designed to generate a more intense degree of psychological realism. They aimed to make the plays seem more cohesive and more plausible in the light of what he took to be their main purpose, the exploration of individual human character as an aspect of a somehow timeless and 'universal' human nature, mysteriously able to transcend the immediate pressures of history, economics and politics. These principles had been fully developed in his influential series of studies called *Prefaces to Shakespeare* which were still appearing at that time.

It is interesting to refer to exactly that moment in the play which has already been mentioned: Lear's peremptory demand 'Give me the map there'. Granville-Barker's concern at this particular point seems, predictably, to have been entirely with Lear's character. In the famous *Preface* to *King Lear* he had already argued that Shakespeare presents Lear's might and genius in the early scenes not in any great series of actions, but 'in every trivial thing that he is'. The production clearly set out to stress this from the first. An eye-witness, Hallam Fordham, makes the general comment that, by contrast with Gielgud's previous performance in the play at the Old Vic in 1931, here 'a clearer definition of character is immediately given and received, unblurred by emotion . . . we have a distinct impression of an old man who is yet alert and masterful; a testy martinet with nerves drawn taut and great enough in himself to be reckoned with.'[16] The details confirm the point:

He walks alone, tall and upright. The carriage of the head indicates a man who takes his absolute authority for granted. The firm tread shows that he is no dotard, although the pace suggests nervous tension . . . As he approaches the foot of the throne his eye lights on Gloucester, standing at the side. Lear pauses, turns half round and strikes the floor impatiently with his staff. The command to attend the suitors is snapped out as an irritable but half-humorous reminder of a duty neglected, and with a swift, disparaging glance after the hastily departing master-of-ceremonies, the King ascends the throne, where he sits with an accustomed ease . . .

There is a second's pause while he flashes a glance at the assembled Court. 'Give me the map there'; without looking he half-extends his hand towards the chamberlain at his side, who puts the roll into it. Scarcely glancing at it, Lear holds the map, still rolled, in his lap and in a formal tone announces his 'fast intent, to shake all cares and business from our age, conferring them on younger strengths.' He points to Albany and Cornwall as he refers to them.[17]

[After Goneril and Regan have spoken]. . . The King is contented. The map is unrolled. Twice the chamberlain kneels to receive it from Lear and holds it while the King indicates the boundaries with a finger which seems to be pointing to the ample lands themselves. The chamberlain holds the map before each of the two elder Princesses in turn, and then returns with it to his place beside the throne. [After Cordelia's refusal to speak] . . . Lear sinks back into his throne, trembling with disappointment and fury at this public rebuke to his pride. At the words 'Let it be so', he snatches the map and holds it crumpled in his hand. . . . His speech disclaiming Cordelia is delivered rapidly, with increasing volume. Kent's expostulation meets with a muttered warning and a terrible glance.

The map is hurled to the ground at the words 'digest the third'. The fatal investment of all his power is made with the utmost speed, and the ceremonial confirmation of the gift rushed through almost contemptuously.

'Without looking he half-extends his hand towards the chamberlain at his side, who puts the roll into it.' We should notice the extent to which this and other gestures, designed to indicate Lear's presupposition of his absolute power, effectively minimize the presence and impact of the map in order to maximize a sense of Lear's individual character and 'personality'. They presume that these have remained unchanged between Shakespeare's time and our own. Yet, in casually draining away three hundred years of history, they also entirely occlude the political dimensions that were surely on offer in the text in 1940 to no less an extent than was the case when the play was first performed.

After all, events at the time of this production certainly pointed towards the possibility of a political and social débâcle at least the equal (bearing in mind the Gunpowder Plot) of that implicit in the Jacobean situation. In both instances, the disintegration of Great Britain as a national state under attack from external forces was quite clearly at issue. In 1940, the material events of the period from 15 April to 25 May mark them as probably the most crucial weeks of recent British history, when the integrity of the state was indeed fundamentally threatened. There was, as people used to remind each other at the time, a war on. It might be helpful to cite some specific events:

15 April (the day the production opened), British and Allied troops landed in occupied Norway (at Narvik) in one of the most disastrous adventures of the war: its failure led directly to the resignation of the British Prime Minister, Neville Chamberlain.

9 May, German troops entered Holland, Belgium and Luxembourg.

10 May, Chamberlain resigned and Winston Churchill became Prime Minister.

14 May, The Allies lost fifty planes and the Germans broke through at Sedan. Many believed their advance would continue through to London.

21 May, Arras and Amiens fell.

23 May, Boulogne fell, Calais was besieged.

25 May, (the day the production closed) fifteen French generals were dismissed. German troops were only 25 miles from the coast of Kent. The first German bombs fell on British soil and the magazine *Picture Post* excitedly announced 'German parachutists must be expected any moment from now on.'

Churchill called the next day, 26 May, 'the blackest day of all'. Calais fell, the Cabinet was splitting, Halifax and Chamberlain recommended suing for peace via Mussolini.

Astonishingly, few of the reviews of the production of *King Lear* connected it with any of these events. *The Times* of 16 April 1940 did make the point that

> To be at the Old Vic last night, waiting in the somewhat dingy but much-liked auditorium for the curtain to rise, was to enjoy a sense of the first genuine theatrical occasion of the war. Occasions of the kind declare themselves not in the sheen of fresh paint, diamonds and gardenias, but in the unmistakable stir of a common intellectual expectancy.

but the rest of the review makes no connection between this 'intellectual expectancy' and events in the wider world. The actors showed a similar capacity for distraction. Speaking of the production, Gielgud later declared:

> It seemed to take our minds *off* the awful things that were happening in France. When people used to come round I would say 'How can you stand seeing so agonizing a play when such terrible things are going on in the world?' and they would answer that it gave them a kind of courage. . . the glory of the play and its magnificent poetry took you out of yourself. Shakespeare has always had that extraordinary appeal for every kind of audience.[18]

Yet in fact this particular audience was also experiencing rather more than a daily threat to the integrity of the kingdom, the deposition of its Prime Minister or even the famous promise made on 13 May 1940, by his successor, of a future which offered nothing but 'blood, toil, tears and sweat' in pursuit of 'victory at all costs'. For instance, they had also witnessed on 22 May (right in the middle of the run of the play) the passing through Parliament, in under three hours, of the Emergency Powers Bill.

This Draconian measure gave the Government virtually unlimited power over all persons and property. Banks and finance came directly under Government control. At the same time, a Treachery Bill established the death penalty for subversive activities. The measures were announced by Clement Attlee in a radio broadcast on the evening of 22 May. 'Today, on your behalf', he proclaimed,

> Parliament has given the Government full power to control all persons and property . . . the services and property of all must be at the disposal of the Government for the common task . . . the Government now has the right to call upon any citizen to do the work that is most immediately required in the national interest.[19]

Many comments might be made on such legislation. Suffice it to say that its immediate effect was revolutionary: suddenly it turned 'us' into 'them', democracy into its opposite. We literally became – for whatever reasons and to whatever effect – what we opposed. But, even more curiously, the Emergency Powers Bill also engendered a rather odd paradox. It took away every vestige of a citizen's individual rights under the law and yet, in its context, it also seemed somehow to be promoting and fostering individuality. The Government even felt able to appeal – on radio, that most individualizing of mediums – to the individual ('Today, on your behalf . . .') as part of the process. Yet at the Old Vic Theatre, with *King Lear* poised to respond to and connect with these complex ironies, nothing seems to have happened. We are in a sense confronted, like Sherlock Holmes, with a dog that didn't bark.

Big time

At this stage, my strategy will be clear enough. By focusing on those 'cultural meanings' that we generate now, in our own historical context – meanings which can hardly be separated from our perception of those generated then, in the text's historical context – I have invoked an aspect of the 'historicism' mentioned earlier. Such an analysis might seem merely practical, in a traditional British mode, at best only of so-called 'academic' interest. But it can also reasonably claim to have broader horizons. In focusing on the way in which different readings of texts compete for the power to generate cultural meaning, and in aiming to see how ideological positions are formed and sustained through their use; how, more specifically, discursive stratagems operate in the criticism and performance of Shakespeare's plays, and on behalf of what and of whom, this sort of analysis commits itself to intervention in matters traditionally thought to lie beyond the walls of the academy. Add an overt concern with the material historical and economic implications of literary criticism itself, together with a focus on the relation between the academic subject called 'English' and the cultural power of the Englishness which it often upholds, and the sense of Cultural Materialism's involvement, at its furthest reach, with larger matters of politics and public policy is unavoidable.

For the British, after all, 'English' never was and never could be just another academic subject. On the contrary, its larger dimension grows directly out of the fact that it was always intended to be *the* subject, both at home and, with perhaps greater significance, abroad: the sacred repository of national values, standards and identity, the crucible in which a whole way of life was to be reverently concocted, shaken, and occasionally stirred. And yet, as recent and continuing stirrings amongst non-English communities in Britain have shown, those on the periphery of this civilizing arrangement, perceived as the non-civilized or Brutish, have a disconcerting habit of periodically dashing that cup from English lips. In the process, perhaps they remind us of the complexity of our inheritance from Brutus, and in its Brutish/British name offer to break free from the smoothing-over process to which a particularly narrow version of 'Englishness' seems committed.

A literary criticism which responds – beyond the boundaries of 'English' – to those peripheral Brutish dimensions might not un-reasonably, as I have suggested, find a sort of rallying point in the work of the late Raymond Williams: a Welshman from the periphery, not an Englishman from the centre, with a lifelong interest in mapping those dimensions of the symbolic boundary-ridden British terrain which his finest novel calls *Border Country*. To such a literary criticism all texts will speak, not of their essential meaning or aesthetic being, but in more mundane social and political terms. They will tell of the uses to which they have been and may be put. As a result, such a criticism will present Shakespeare, say, as an agency of cultural meaning, see his plays as potential political weapons, and 'English' as an ideological stratagem, one of the most insidious forms of boundary-building and map-mongering colonization, its ultimate aim perhaps the establishment, reinforcement and camouflaging of paradoxes such as that concerning individuality which we have already identified as stalking the stage of the Old Vic Theatre in London in 1940.

Foucault would see such a contradiction as part and parcel of a larger project, designed to enlist a society's subjects in the process of their own subjection. As Paul Rabinow coldly puts it,

> The power of the state to produce an increasingly totalizing web of control is intertwined with and dependent on its ability to produce an increasing specification of individuality.[20]

Granville-Barker's production of *King Lear*, a play which surely focuses to a considerable degree on the British state and its involvement with a totalizing web of control, offers a good example of this process in action. The production's over-busy concern with a particular 'specification of individuality', Lear's personality, systematically deflects rather than engages with the larger issues at work, both in Shakespeare's time and in 1940, which invite an audience to *produce* meaning from the play rather than passively ingest it. The map of Britain, that almost Brechtian text which speaks eloquently from within the first scene and comments, silently but ironically, on Lear's pretensions throughout, is accordingly reduced by Granville-Barker to the level of a mere prop used to point up an aspect of individual 'character'.

The result is that this *King Lear* offered not an engagement with politics but a diversion from them. If it 'took you out of yourself', it did so paradoxically, as part of its reinforcement of the fundamental primacy of individual selfhood. And yet it also manages, in a contradictory mode almost the equal of the tragic oxymoron of Lear's divisive kingship, to endorse the obliteration of individual selfhood precisely whilst reinforcing it. As the King reaches for the map, his 'personalizing' gesture brings the consolations of a phantom individuality to its by now wholly de-individualized, standardized, conscripted, weighed, measured, rationed, uniformed, disenfranchised, shaven-headed and thoroughly 'subjected' wartime audience. But such a gesture, such a production, hardly *contests* their condition or the totalizing thrust of the Emergency Powers Bill which confirms it. On the contrary, and in context, it positively *enables* that measure, makes it acceptable, and, by taking its audience 'out of' themselves, would have effectively served to stifle any questioning of it. After all, is it not to defend just this, *King Lear* at the Old Vic, that we are fighting? The emergency powers and their web of control seem momentarily not to undermine but somehow almost to bolster our

English heritage, a heritage vested in an academic subject called 'English', of which the Bard is ironically by this time the very linchpin.

In short, far from challenging or engaging with that contradiction, this *King Lear* can be said to have been wholly complicit with it. I am not, of course, referring to the play itself. No 'play itself' is ever available to us. I am referring once again to the process whereby, particularly in times of crisis, a society 'means by' a work of art. The Gielgud–Granville-Barker production of *King Lear* – certainly on that evening of 22 May 1940, when the announcement of the Emergency Powers Bill is made, perhaps most intensely at that very moment when Lear's personalizing reaching for the map might even have coincided with Attlee's depersonalizing reaching for the microphone – offers a powerful instance, if not emblem, of the whole business.

Whirligig

By now, Granville-Barker too had an almost emblematic dimension: one of tragic Shakespearean proportions. His decline had begun in 1916 at the tercentenary of Shakespeare's death, when it became clear that the National Theatre, for which he had strenuously campaigned, was further away than at any other time in his life. Instead, the musical *Chu Chin Chow* opened in London in August 1916 and ran for five years.

The effect on him was disastrous. He writes (in *Exemplary Theatre*, 1922) of the 'bitterness of my realization . . . of the theatre's utter and ignominious failure during the [First World] War to lift its head into any region of fine feeling and eloquence.' Presumably in pursuit of these qualities, he joined the British Military Intelligence Service in October 1916 and worked in that capacity at the War Office until the end of hostilities. In 1918 he married again, this time a rich American, Helen Huntingdon, and effectively abandoned his theatrical kingdom. One biographer called him 'a hero who gave up the struggle, threw off the dust of battle and became a mere Professor'.[21] He then took to his study (his wife felt that writing was more genteel a pursuit than the theatre) and prepared the way for an audience that was sure to be mainly concerned with particular 'specifications of individuality' by the writing of his immensely influential *Prefaces to Shakespeare*: works which focus centrally on the construction of a sense of individuality and which, by their success, fuelled the mass development of the academic subject 'English' that further fostered and institutionalized it.

Nevertheless, the whirligig of time brings in his revenges. In 1940, Granville-Barker's home was in Paris. Throughout the rehearsals for *King Lear*, his wife had been sending urgent messages to him in London chronicling the inexorable approach of the enemy. Lear-like, the man who had abandoned his theatrical kingdom sought still to retain a foothold in it, and the rehearsals (which he was conducting virtually in secrecy) continued almost up to the first night. That darker purpose nevertheless failed. The winds blew and cracked their cheeks. Paris fell in June 1940. Granville-Barker escaped to America (once again working for the British Government – at one stage the British Council – in a mysterious capacity). But the map of his Europe was decisively rolled up, and would not be needed again in his, or indeed our, lifetime.

But that is not really the end of the matter. This essay has of course presented Granville-Barker as a latter-day King Lear: one whose 'division' of his own life had cut him off from the 'real' Cordelia-like Shakespeare who represents self-present, self-evident transparent Truth, and who, in consequence, finds himself committed to the false Gonerils and Regans of 'English'. It might be said to have constructed a kind of biographical fallacy which 'personalizes' what is really a larger and more complex historical/cultural process. It might even be said to have 'demonized' Granville-Barker and his 1940 production, on the spurious grounds that a 'public' or 'political' reading of the play is 'truer', more close to the 'original' Shakespeare, than his twentieth-century 'private' or 'individualized' version. I would argue nevertheless that there are some reasonable grounds for offering him as a representative figure and for using his biography as an operative 'myth'. His work after all (particularly the *Prefaces to Shakespeare*) remains enormously influential, and in respect of recent critical approaches to Shakespeare, he can stand as a satisfactorily established adversary. Nevertheless, the fundamental opposition which has apparently been proposed,

True Shakespeare   v. False 'Shakespeare'
(political/communal)   v. (psychological/individual)

can hardly bear a great deal of looking into for the following reasons:

(a) The notion of a self-present, 'unified subject' Shakespeare, the originator of transparently 'true' texts, is deeply suspect: in no instance more so than that presented by the case of *King Lear*. There are after all *two* 'organically distinct' texts of the play, the Quarto and the Folio versions, not one: a situation now recognized by the editors of the Oxford edition of the plays, who have scandalously

published both.[22] If we allow for modern 'conflations' of these, it means that in our time there have always been at least *three* extant texts of the play. In short, Shakespeare himself can be said, Lear-like, to have divided his own kingdom: to have produced a textual 'map' which reduces and shatters the unity the present essay finds itself defending. If Granville-Barker can be called Lear, so can William Shakespeare.

(b) The claim that Granville-Barker's *King Lear*, with its individualized, character-led bearing, offers no political reading of the play is also shaky. In fact, that production puts forward a highly politicized reading of the text: one which ranks as deeply conservative (even today) and which of course accords well with official British propaganda versions of the last war (fought to preserve individual liberties, etc.). Among the audience, potentially if not actually, we might even have been able to glimpse the critic E. M. W. Tillyard, whose intensely, albeit covertly, political *The Elizabethan World Picture* must at that time have begun its germination (it was published in 1943).

(c) This essay's own account of the situation itself presents a divisive map whereby, Lear-like, its author divides a conceptual kingdom between a Cordelia (True Shakespeare) and a Goneril/Regan (False 'Shakespeare'). This places him at one with Granville-Barker and (perhaps not unhappily) with the Bard. Map-makers all. And that, perhaps, may be allowed to prompt a further thought:

(d) The opposition 'real world/mapped world; actual terrain/virtual terrain' with which I began, and which runs in a sense throughout my argument, must itself be entirely questionable. It is, surely, a version of other fundamentally dubious oppositions, such as Nature/Culture, and Speech/Writing. They are dubious because it is Culture after all that *produces* Nature. It is Writing that *determines* our perception of Speech and perhaps presents its essential character. It is the map that *constitutes* the terrain rather than simply describing or representing it. There are no 'real', material, unmapped, uncharted terrains, just as, of course, there are no objective mappings of them – despite the characteristic attempts, say, of the Victorians with their 'Ordnance Survey' maps of Great Britain: a massively reductive and controlling exercise aptly linked by name to the military teams that undertook it. For map-making is surely one of those material cultural practices by which, quite as much as with plays, novels and poems, we produce (and impose) meaning. 'Meaning by' invests all our activity. To live is to make maps (or texts). To make maps is to mean. To term a terrain 'unmapped' or 'uncharted' is only to map or chart it, and thus to 'mean by' it, in a particular way.

It is, of course, permissible to argue that some maps are more progressive than others. However, since that assertion takes place within the context of the strategies of New Historicism and Cultural Materialism, as I have outlined them here, some reflections on those developments must finally be appropriate. For it would be misleading, as well as clearly against the fundamental tenets of this sort of approach, to suggest that the project in which both are involved is watertight, complete, and devoid of serious difficulties. Far from it. If Cultural Materialism, for instance, were not itself permanently in process, it would have been overtaken by a serious contradiction. The problems any such programmes face are many and, amongst others, the following seem of particular importance:

(e) The position from which both New Historicism and Cultural Materialism argue risks being compromised by the argument itself. Thus, if all cultures can and must be 'historicized', and if their natures and concerns ultimately turn out to be unwittingly tailored to and unconsciously imprisoned by the economic, social and political pressures of their age and their way of life, then so is our own. Future historians will no doubt effortlessly demonstrate that, far from at last presenting the 'truth' about Shakespearean drama, both New Historicism and Cultural Materialism are enterprises which, as products of our current Western European or North American presuppositions, prove to be as blindly culture-specific as the societies they describe. However, this is only a disabling factor if we persist in regarding the attainment of permanent, transhistorical truth as the object of the exercise. If we abandon that goal, then once the limitations of both methods are recognized, they become aspects of a self-knowledge which valuably sharpens the process of reading and even helps the reader towards a more telling purchase on its purpose in the current and continuing debate which facilitates the construction and reconstruction of our own world.

(f) Positivism remains a recurrent spectre. As part of their project of seeking out precise moments of potential contradiction and subversion, both New Historicists and Cultural Materialists have to argue that a reservoir of anti-humanism, with an associated tendency to decentredness and fragmented subjectivity, has an objective existence in Elizabethan society, and is not merely the product of a particular mode of reading.[23] This seems to be a path which might ultimately lead to the mere replacement of one Elizabethan World Picture by another. The position is again partly retrievable to the extent that Cultural Materialism's motives are at least clear. Its final interest in the use we make of Shakespeare in our own world is usually firmly declared. And that makes all the difference in so far as its aim is thus not simply to describe the past 'as it was'. It is, rather, polemically to re-read, re-narrate, and so re-claim the past in the name of the construction of a more acceptable present. The assumption that this is a feasible project in which all societies continually engage rests on principles which are hardly those of positivism.

(g)   For a culture to exist at all, and to be meaningful to itself, it will always need to establish principles of subordination, marginalization, and peripheralization. Language itself works by such means. The nature of the phoneme indicates that exclusion is necessary in order to make meaning. Is the idea of pluralism, or the wholesale abandonment of exclusion – sometimes seemingly advocated by Cultural Materialism – therefore merely sentimental?[24] Can it not be asked of any text in any culture, whose voice is being silenced in order that it may speak? Is it enough for the cultural analyst to expose the relation of dominant and subordinated or silenced voices? Isn't some imperative also implied? And doesn't this land us ultimately with the problem of moral choice? Do we not finally have to choose which voices are to be silenced? If the answer is yes, it can only be justified on the understanding that the question will be repeatedly asked, that the answer will be regularly scrutinized, and that the sort of cultural interrogation it implies will be constantly carried out. Cultural Materialism and New Historicism ought, in some degree, to be guarantors of that sort of vigilance. At the very least, this should be among the first issues to be raised whenever a modern Lear, beginning the latest round of divisive cuts, calls ominously for a map to be brought before him.

7 Bardbiz[1]

Few things unhinge the British as much as doublet and hose. The merest hint unleashes golden fantasies of order and well-being, yoking together gentility and free-born earthiness within a deep dream of peace. And so, in 1989, when bulldozers in Southwark accidentally laid bare the foundations first of the Rose Theatre and then of the Globe, a furore began fit to astonish any passing Elizabethan ghost. The possibility that one of these sites might fall prey to property developers generated more squeaking and gibbering in the London streets than you could shake a severed head at. Greenrooms of actors ranged anoraked bodies against the pile-drivers. Guggenheims of scholars jumboed in from North America. There was weeping and wailing and the gnashing of clapper boards for the TV cameras. The air thickened with pronouncements about culture, art and our 'national heritage'.

It's worth reminding ourselves during the present lull in hostilities that a salutary strand of Puritanism is woven into the very 'national heritage' that the self-appointed guardians of the Rose and the Globe Theatres claim to be preserving. One of the major charges levelled by the Puritans against the playhouses of Shakespeare's day was that they were involved in and encouraged idolatry: the worship of graven images. The appalling spectacle of famous actors and actresses actually praying over heaps of bricks and mortar, lighting candles and tying paper flowers to the wire fencing around the Rose and the Globe, had a familiar whiff.

Andrew Gurr and John Orrell's *Rebuilding Shakespeare's Globe* concerns a project conceived well before the recent discoveries. But its primary aim – to present the case for a 'reconstruction' of the Globe Theatre in Southwark near the site of the original – might well set the odd Puritan nostril twitching. Gurr's crisp, lucid survey of the present state of knowledge about audiences, acting companies and playgoing in 1600 is predictably impeccable and nothing less could be said of Orrell's account of the structure of the original Globe and the Inigo Jones designs for indoor theatres. The book's scholarship, its commitment, its good intentions lie manifestly beyond dispute. However, there are difficulties.

The first and most obvious one lurks in the linked notions of 'reconstruction' and 'original'. Their involvement in what the fell sergeants of deconstruction have urged us to see as a culture-specific need to establish legitimating presences and what less ambitious citizens might rank as a longing for a vanished Eden, should give us pause here. The potential of 'origin' as an agent of affirmation, confirmation and limitation makes it a powerful ideological tool. If we can persuade ourselves that in some way origins generate authenticity, determine, establish and reinforce essentials, then we can forget about change and about the history and politics which produce it. A covert, idolatrous agenda backs temptingly into view. The 'original' Globe Theatre! That firmest of rocks on which the true unchanging English culture is founded! To bolt the shifting uncertain present firmly to that monument must be a project worth encouraging. Let Europe loom, the pound wilt, Shakespeare's wooden O offers a peculiarly satisfying bulwark against change.

Another difficulty is that the notion of an 'original' Globe Theatre doesn't bear much looking into. There were, to begin with, two of them. The first Globe was constructed in 1599. It burned down in 1613 and a second Globe was constructed on the same site. If the first Globe is the 'original' one, then a central problem must be that the timbers from which it was built were themselves 'originally' used to construct Burbage's first playhouse, called The Theatre, situated on the north bank of the Thames and dismantled in December 1598. In short, the first and 'original' Globe was itself already a literal 'reconstruction' of a pre-existing theatre and the present project runs the serious risk of being a reconstruction of a reconstruction. The dizzying prospect of a third remove enters with the fact that the best physical picture of the Globe is the one afforded by Wenceslas Hollar's 'Long View' of London. But this gives a view of the second Globe, which is of course a reconstruction on the same site of the first Globe. Finally, as if in mockery of all such reaching after authenticity, it happens that Hollar's engraving reverses the captions on the two buildings, with the result that the one it clearly nominates as 'The Globe' is no such thing. Indeed, the sacred edifice itself is ignominiously designated for all to see as an arena for 'Beere bayting'.

The less than edifying spectacle of scholars in pursuit of authenticity is familiar enough in the field of Shakespearean textual scholarship, where the quest for what the Bard 'originally' wrote in pristine and unsullied manuscript form has its own comic and ideologically illuminating history. But Gurr and Orrell's meticulous and delicate work deserves a better fate than the underwriting of what has begun to look rather like an Elizabethan theme park with two reconstructed playhouses (the Globe and the 'Inigo Jones playhouse') firmly (if that's the word) at its centre – I speak as a former enthusiast for the project. The playhouses, we are told, will act as the focus of a larger complex, an 'educational milieu' no less, presenting a 'recreated piece of London's history'. The good news is that, to conform to modern fire regulations, the theatres will have illuminated Exit signs. Light one for me.

There is of course an ultimate difficulty. What can never be reconstructed is the major ingredient of all Shakespeare's plays, the factor which completed them and made them work: their original audience. Annabel Patterson's *Shakespeare and the Popular Voice* boldly confronts this issue in a spirited study of the ways in which the plays might be said to give that audience a voice. Rejecting as 'counter-intuitive' the notion that Shakespeare would have supported an aristocratic and 'anti-popular' myth of society, she offers instead a populist Bard writing on the side of an inherited cultural tradition of popular protest. But by the early nineteenth century this Shakespeare had been expunged from the record and a different voice was on offer as the true utterance of the Bard. Patterson is one of a number of critics and scholars who have recently been trying either to establish contact with the voice of the earlier incarnation or to understand the nature of the expunging process itself.

One of the most effective agents in that respect was certainly the apostate Coleridge, whose lectures on Shakespeare gear themselves to a growing fear of popular revolution and, in the playwright's name, deploy a considered programme of anti-Jacobin propaganda. As Jonathan Bate has recently pointed out in an incisive study of the cultural politics of the period, *Shakespearean Constitutions: Politics, Theatre, Criticism 1730–1830*, Hazlitt stands as the Radical to Coleridge's Conservative in terms of a struggle for possession of Shakespeare that was a feature of British ideology between Waterloo and Peterloo.

Shakespeare's centrality as an instrument of cultural meaning was confirmed by that contest. The creature familiar to us as 'Shakespeare' was to some degree produced by it. Reinforced and transmitted by the educational system, this is a figure we immediately recognize and embrace: liberal, disinterested, all-wise, his plays the repository, guarantee and chief distributor next to God of unchanging truth. If there is a darker side, it emerges in the conclusion to which Hazlitt is ineluctably drawn – that Shakespeare is ultimately complicit by virtue of his poetic imagination with the political power he scrutinizes.

Bate's thoughtful analysis suggests that the plays ultimately elude wholesale appropriation, that they cannot be finally constituted by political preference. But Hazlitt's conclusion remains to trouble us. Are Shakespeare's plays *essentially* reactionary? Can we discern popular protest only in their unconscious revelations, in the patterns of their systematic blindness? Or do they offer us the direct voice of that protest, once we have trained ourselves to hear it beyond the filtering mediations of the intervening years?

In Annabel Patterson's view, this 'direct voice' comes to us indirectly through a kind of 'ventriloquism', whenever we hear it cited by its enemies on the stage. *A Midsummer Night's Dream* offers a good example. If we move beyond the operatic and balletic accretions attached to the play between 1662 (when Pepys was able to dismiss it as 'the most insipid ridiculous play that ever I saw in my life') and 1914 (when Granville-Barker tried to dispense with the scenic display that generations of spectacular musical versions had imposed), 'the play that Shakespeare wrote' emerges in a powerful and startlingly different light.

The major beneficiary of such a re-vision is the character of Bottom, with the production of *Pyramus and Thisbe* in which he stars thrust by it into new prominence. This mocking and sharply focused performance – capable of making its aristocratic audience as uncomfortable as the performance of *The Mousetrap* does in *Hamlet* – takes up virtually the whole of the fifth Act of the play and the rehearsals for it resonate throughout the rest of the action to such a degree that they drown out much of the rather tedious, framing plot. Add factors such as the Oxfordshire rising of 1596 and the midsummer disturbances in London of 1595 (involving up to a thousand rioters, a mixture of artisans and apprentices) and the worrying potential of the presence on the stage of a number of such persons becomes apparent. Bottom's repeated assurances that he and his men have no wish to cause alarm is an example of the 'ventriloquism' Patterson cites. His sexual triumph with Titania – an enactment in fantasy of upper-class fears regarding the potency of the lower elements both of society and the body – is another.

In this way, Patterson argues, the play engages effectively with the political pressures operative in its society. Whether or not – in its 'carnival' or 'festive' mode – it aspires to defuse them is of course another matter. Early modern 'festival' occasions, with their ritual mocking of authority, are said nowadays to have functioned largely as 'safety valves' for harshly repressed communities. But many instances exist in which their subversive potential seems to have taken over the occasion and turned it into a political manifestation of some power, if no precise focus. Our own experience of so-called 'football violence' may well interest future historians on this basis. But Patterson argues that it was not until after the Midlands Rising of 1607 'that Shakespeare was forced to admit that the popular voice had grievances that the popular theatre could no longer express comedically'.

As a result, that voice gradually becomes more direct and less 'ventriloquized'. *Hamlet* marks the point of transition to the new dynamics of the reign of James. As the Prince increasingly uses the terms employed by artisans and the lower orders, he seems to commit himself to a language learned from the politically voiceless, and thus to become their mouthpiece. To the court this signifies madness.

Madness of a similar sort characterizes those speeches of Lear which seem to offer a radical critique of a social structure in which men can change places 'handy dandy' because no social position has absolute standing. In this play, says Patterson, Shakespeare overtly takes up the case of society's victims and – in a startling, transgressive gesture – boldly confronts a monarch with them.

But the 'frontal political nakedness' of *Coriolanus* makes it the obvious focal point of her analysis. Of course, the same feature also accounts for the degree of ideological appropriation which has ever been this play's lot. Marxist and Fascist readings have tugged at it repeatedly. Both Charlotte Brontë's *Shirley* and George Eliot's *Felix Holt* have processed it for their own purposes. The play seems always to have functioned as a kind of arena. However, Patterson's concern to establish what the 'text of *Coriolanus* itself' has to say presumes to stand aside from all this in an attempt to read the actual 'grain' of the play in its own terms. In her view, it offers a pro-democratic analysis of the strengths and weaknesses of republican political theory, which it presents as a challenge to the authoritarian principles underpinning the Jacobean state. Of course, as she points out, to choose a Roman subject was in any case to engage in a Jacobean cultural practice which had its own oppositional 'grain'. Hobbes himself warned that 'they that live under a Monarch conceive an opinion, that the Subjects in a Popular Commonwealth enjoy Liberty; but that in a Monarchy they are all Slaves'.[2] But this fails to account for the sheer clout of the plebeian's case, its political acumen, its grasp of the strategies of patrician argument, its tough-minded capacity for counter-attack. Under Patterson's admirably intense scrutiny, the play appears to raise the fundamental populist questions of who should speak for the commons, what power the common people should have in the system, and the extent to which such power is compatible with national safety.

Problems arise of course with the claim that these are the 'real' and essential meanings of the text 'itself', the heart of the 'play that Shakespeare wrote', the standard from which other readings diverge. The account she herself supplies of the various uses made of *Coriolanus* in history creates particular difficulties for Patterson's brand of essentialism because it indicates that no text is wholly obdurate, hardened into single meaning. The opposite case can be just as persuasively put. It would argue that texts yield only to reading and that reading is a political and a politicizing act; that to read a text, in however complex a mode, is to enlist it. In terms of material practice there can be no final 'text itself', floating free from current and previous processing. And paradoxically, in the event, the supple power of Patterson's own readings helps to make this point.

Her project – the reclamation of Shakespeare in the name of the common people – has an attractive urgency that the sophistication of current critical theories should not be permitted simply to dismiss. Her scholarship is never less than scrupulous, adroitly deployed and deftly driven home by close attention to the text. She has valiantly sifted a mass of historical material and future generations will thank her for that and for her efforts, signalled by reiterated attention to a set of metaphors involving heels, toes and shoeleather, to keep all our feet firmly on the ground.

Nevertheless, the main difficulty with her argument lies less in its presentation of the plays as the 'expression' of a popular voice, than in its conviction that, in this, they represent the unmediated fulfilment of their author's intentions. If Shakespeare's plays can be said to be more (and less) than this, it is primarily because they are texts, and thus constituted not only by an author but also by the interpretive strategies of readers and the material political and social pressures of the historical contexts helping to shape those strategies. That processing has at the least made the 'plays themselves' unreachable. At best, it may itself be more interesting and more revealing than they could ever be.

For it is surely the case that we can have no immediate or objective access to the works of an 'essential' Shakespeare, to the 'plays themselves', or to what they 'really' mean. Nor could Shakespeare. Indeed, that is hardly the point of him or them. The point of Shakespeare and his plays lies in their capacity to serve as instruments by which we make cultural meaning for ourselves. In short, we can say of Shakespeare's plays what we can say of those other instruments by which we make meaning, the words of our language. They don't, in themselves, 'mean'. It is *we* who mean, *by* them.

In just this spirit, Gary Taylor's *Reinventing Shakespeare* offers a lively 'cultural history' of our use of the Bard. In fact, he proposes a new discipline somewhat clumsily dubbed 'Shakesperotics', whose field is more or less everything that a culture gets up to in the name of Shakespeare. Taylor's quarry is that by now transnational cultural and commercial industry whose product's potency underwrites the appearance of its emblem on banknotes, pub-signs, credit cards, T-shirts. What Shakesperotics confronts could well be termed Bardbiz.

Taylor takes up the story from 1660, the point at which the theatres reopened, but ironically also the point by which most material knowledge of Shakespeare and his plays had been lost. The whole subsequent history of Shakespearean scholarship, criticism and performance is the story of that knowledge's retrieval or, better to stress the age's purposeful employment of the Bard, its 'restoration'. For restoring Shakespeare after 1660 links him to the restored monarchy, the House of Lords and the Anglican Church – to the mutual advantage of each. Meaning *by* Shakespeare even awards *Pericles*, an inherently unlikely choice, a brief toehold in the Restoration repertoire because it can be made to speak to the adventures of Charles II. In much the same way, *Henry V* offers itself as a vehicle for the mediation of wartime trauma. In our own century, Olivier's film addresses the Allied invasion of Normandy in 1944 and – perhaps more obliquely – Kenneth Branagh's film engages with the current carnage of Belfast.

In the eighteenth century an early shift of emphasis from performance to print led to Shakespeare's becoming irrevocably woven into the strands of a national literary culture, first through long-standing discussion of the plays in *The Spectator* and *The Tatler*, and then as a result of Jacob Tonson's practice of persuading well-known writers to edit the Bard's works. For over a century, some of the finest authors in English merged their talents with those of Shakespeare as they helped in the remodelling and transmission of his plays; always a good investment as the increasing number of editions of the *Complete Works* shows. Taylor calculates that in the hundred years up to 1708, there were four of them. In the following hundred years, there were sixty-five. Nor need we dismiss this activity as barren. Poetry itself springs from the search for what Shakespeare actually wrote when, with Pope's *Dunciad*, a master-piece by one interpreter of Shakespeare grows out of an attack on two others, Theobald and Cibber.

If Bardbiz took root at the beginning of the eighteenth century, it was in full flower at its close. The Romantics, who might have challenged the Shakespearean hegemony, ended by colluding with it in the interest of the preservation of a national culture. Part of the effect of the French Revolution in Britain was, as Leigh Hunt remarked, 'to endear the nation to its own habits'. Amongst these was a mistrust of rational abstraction and a preference for intuitive, organic development. Led by Coleridge's organicist political theories transmuted to a theory of aesthetics, Romanticism tended to glorify the Shakespearean canon as the benignly rule-flouting, coherence-generating, meaning-conferring work of a genuinely British Bard. 'Chief Poet!' Keats called him, sitting down to read *King Lear* again, 'Begetter of our deep eternal theme!' Unlike revolutionary France and America, Britain entered the nineteenth century without the benefit of a rationalized, written Constitution. But in terms of making meaning, the works of the Chief Poet served as well if not better.

Victorian processing of that Constitution benefited from scholarly work on Biblical texts and indeed from parallel developments in science and industry. Division of labour brought precision in dating, ordering, collating. In 1864 a watershed was reached. For in that year the aptly named Globe edition of the plays appeared and remained the ubiquitous standard text for over a century. Produced by three Cambridge dons, it marked the first serious entry into Bardbiz of professional academic 'experts'. Fighting off the attempted depreda-tions of marauding Baconians, scholars such as Edward Dowden (one of the first human beings ever to earn his living by teaching Shakespeare), related the plays to an imaginary, Darwinesque, smoothly evolutionary 'life' of the playwright whose narrative embodied many of the age's presuppositions concerning history, psychology, and the nature of the subtly progressive English-speaking world whose imperial hub was London.

Dowden was an Anglo-Irish Protestant and his *Shakspere: A Critical Study of His Mind and Art* (which went through twelve British editions between 1875 and 1901 and is still in print) not unnaturally discerns in the Bard's life and works a covert scenario for the settlement of the

Irish problem. But what such studies overtly achieved was the shepherding of Shakespeare into the examination room. There, with the additional help of such as the rogue philosopher A. C. Bradley, the rapidly developing academic subject called 'English' – addressed to readers of the plays, not theatre-goers – used Shakespeare as a kingpin in its project of welding native cultures abroad and local cultures at home into a single coherent imperial entity.

Taylor's racy populism makes no bones about pointing to the professional academics as themselves the creators of the problem-racked Bard they currently study. He rips into their pretensions with relish, partly by making the point that by the clear light of day the subject of them turns out to be a writer of no necessary distinction: a former star, reduced now to the status of a 'black hole'. By the middle of the twentieth century, firmly in the possession of research-minded professors and indeed the staple of many of their careers, Shake-speare appeared to speak only the *patois* of Modernism. As intimate with foreign cultures as Joyce, as widely read as Pound, as laden with literary references as Eliot, his failure to produce *The Waste Land*, *Ulysses* or the *Cantos* was merely an oversight. Indeed, an extra nick from Taylor's finely honed irony is reserved for Cleanth Brooks, whose essay 'Shakespeare as a Symbolist poet' (1945, reprinted as 'The Naked Babe and the Cloak of Manliness' in *The Well Wrought Urn* in 1947) seems to epitomize the academic profession at its most self-serving.

Finally, the focus narrows to 1986, the year of the World Shake-speare Congress in Berlin. It finds Taylor jetting to major centres of Bardbiz in London, Chicago, Oxford, Stratford, Washington, Paris and elsewhere, offering *en route* a tough-guy run-down on the scholars and critics operating in each place. Who would have thought the Bard had undone so many? Pale groaning shades slink past: feminists, bibliographers, theatre-historians, Marxists, historic-ists new and old. Some wretched 'white British Shakespearean scholar', scourged in half a paragraph for a lifetime's imperception, is well on his chastened way back to the sulphurous and tormenting flames before I realize that he bears my own name. This is Bardbiz, nor are we out of it.

Neither is Taylor. For 1986 is also the year which sees the unveiling of the *Oxford Shakespeare*, of which he is himself an editor. Oxford, Shakespeare, the words chime an authoritative peal. But the Ameri-can Taylor is quick to suggest that the revolutionary modes they ring in (the disintegrationist Oxford edition prints two distinct versions of *King Lear* and is as genuinely 'shocking' to some as any Marxist or

Deconstructionist accounts of the plays) are underwritten and perhaps compromised by the global prestige of the institutions from which they spring.

Nevertheless, there's no people like Bardbiz People and, on the strength of this volume, the star that has been hung on Gary Taylor's study door need not be revoked just yet. No black hole he. His sprightly 'March of Time' style, his cheeky, know-all stance, his gamy psychopathology of academic life, will win him few cigars in academe, where it's all right to be a star, but not all right to want it so much. The book's central weakness – its under-theorized commitment to a 'real' (albeit unremarkable) Shakespeare lying underneath all the 'reinventions' – shouldn't be permitted to spoil the fun. For in what amounts to a case study of the contingencies that determine social renown and political influence, Taylor has found a novel way to place a sensitive and scholarly finger on the pulse of our culture. Like it or not, this tightly-packed, incisive and often infuriating book represents a genuine contribution to our knowledge of how that culture works.

For a lot of people, it works by the deployment of power in specific interests and through covert channels. Taylor's book is not the first to suggest that literature acts as one of these, but the recent republication of influential books by Malcolm Evans and Jonathan Dollimore confirms a developing and converging set of concerns with the possibilities, the subtleties and the crudities of the process he spotlights. Although Evans's *Signifying Nothing*, a virtuoso performance of startling ingenuity, is very different from Dollimore's edgy, penetrative and disconcerting *Radical Tragedy*, both have had important roles to play in a continuing revisionary project which in the last decade or so has aimed at a reassessment of Shakespeare and Elizabethan drama precisely in terms of that connection with politics.

Fundamentally, the project has involved locating the drama in history. First, by re-inserting the plays into the cultural history of their own time, by abandoning the modern category of 'literature' and merging them back into the context of the circulating discourses from which 'English' has prised them, it sets out to judge the degree to which the drama was or was not complicit with the powers of the state that seem to sustain it. Second, by inserting the 'afterlives' of the plays into subsequent history and by historicizing salient features of 'literature' and 'criticism', it offers to assess their use as instruments of present cultural meaning.

The first enterprise seems largely to have sprung from American spoil where, as 'New Historicism', it has for some time been subjecting the historical 'meaning' of Elizabethan drama in its own time to extensive realignment. The second is a mostly British phenomenon and comes partly in response to a more abrasive political climate. Despite a certain amount of uneasy fidgeting beneath a common banner whose strange device reads 'Cultural Materialism', much of its activity remains most fruitfully grounded in the work of Raymond Williams. Both Evans and Dollimore offer powerful examples of the unsettling purchase this newly historicized and politicized British criticism can obtain on the Elizabethan past and the post-Thatcher-ized present. Latterly, British concerns have started to make their presence more strongly felt in the United States and in Hugh H. Grady's *The Modernist Shakespeare: Critical Texts in a Material World*, the ideological underpinnings and the literary and politicial roots of academic literary criticism on both sides of the Atlantic are at the centre of the stage.

Indeed, it is mildly surprising that Gary Taylor himself fails to burst from the wings in the most recent example of what might be termed American Cultural Materialism, Michael Bristol's fascinating *Shakespeare's America, America's Shakespeare*. Taylor's nationality, his co-editorship of the *Oxford Shakespeare*, to say nothing of his capacity for discovering 'new' poems by the Bard (the best forgotten 'Shall I Die?') identify him as one of that indefatigable army who have astonishingly established a British playwright as a central institutional feature of the way of life of the United States.

However, Bristol's book complements Taylor's and to some extent neatly outflanks it by means of a much harder-hitting and more consciously stressed political dimension. The result is a trenchant materialist account of the way Shakespeare has been and is being used within American culture. Bristol's examination of the epistemo-logical implications of the topic has an appropriate depth. But there is a level at which the issue is also very simple: Shakespeare functions as one of the central ways in which America makes itself meaningful in its own eyes. And at the heart of that there is a clear anomaly: deep inside the New World's project of *renovatio* lies a commitment to the Old World so powerful that it seeps into the very foundations and institutions of the Republic.

Bristol begins by subjecting the theoretical bases of current Shake-speare studies to devastating scrutiny. Their effects are well known: Shakespeare as timeless, 'beyond ideology', the centre and epitome of that 'affirmative culture' which humanism tirelessly promotes. The causes are pursued and disentangled in areas such as the political economy of scholarship within the educational apparatus, the use of 'tradition' as a social agency, and the employment of bibliographical and editing techniques in the 'deuteronomic' reconstruction of an originating 'authority'.

Concrete detail enlivens the story. The diary of John Adams – one of the founding fathers of the Republic – records a melancholy trip he made to Stratford in 1786 in the company of Thomas Jefferson. The Americans cut slivers from an old chair in which Shakespeare had supposedly sat and, beginning a tradition to which Henry James and T. S. Eliot were heirs, proceeded to admonish the bemused locals on their ignorance of their own heritage. Just how and why a society founded on and committed to distrust of hereditary privilege, and holding sacred the principle that, in Adams's words, 'real merit should govern the world', managed to cleave to its very bosom an artist whose primary themes are, as Bristol says, 'the pathos of kingship and the decline of the great feudal classes' constitutes the puzzle his book sets out to solve. In the process, a chilling thesis emerges: the interpretation of Shakespeare and the interpretation of American political culture are mutually determining practices.

A simpler, if no less disturbing way of putting it is to say that Shakespeare has become, both metaphorically and literally, an American institution. A major symbol of this is the Folger Shakespeare Library. One of the world's great collections of Shakespeareana, it was founded by Henry Clay Folger, President of Standard Oil. Rejecting suggestions that it be housed in Stratford-upon-Avon, Folger insisted that his library should be situated in close proximity to the Supreme Court, the Library of Congress, and other edifices in the heart of Washington DC. When it opened in 1932, Joseph Quincy Adams spoke of Shakespeare's establishment as 'the cornerstone of cultural discipline' in America at a time when 'the forces of immigration became a menace to the preservation of our long-established English civilization'. Indeed, in his speech at Folger's funeral, William Slade, the Library's first Director, made this symbolism explicit by pointing out that

> [A] line drawn from the site of the Folger Shakespeare Memorial through the Capitol building and extended onward, will all but touch the monument to Washington and the memorial to Lincoln.

Washington, Lincoln, Shakespeare: the Bard as the completing element of democracy's Holy Trinity and bulwark against the alien hordes is no more ludicrous an idea than many encountered in Bristol's provocative study. Put with verve and wit, his case has disconcerting implications for defenders of Britain's own no less rickety and probably no more long-established 'English civilization'.

The centrality of Shakespeare to American culture – indeed, the function of his work as a central site of cultural struggle there – might finally make us look again at the Globe Theatre project in London. Its onlie begetter is of course an American, the talented actor Sam Wanamaker, and the project owes most of its success to his transatlantic vigour. If the pile rising in Southwark silently berates the locals for neglecting their heritage, perhaps it not only evokes the shades of Adams and Jefferson on their visit to Stratford, but also shares certain features of other rather more threatening transatlantic missions periodically set up in our midst. Of course, they all offer to defend our way of life. They would, wouldn't they? Is Bardbiz in this guise merely the continuation of American foreign policy by other means? The praying actors might ponder that. Meanwhile, a line drawn across the road from the original location of Shakespeare's wooden O, not more than a fret and a strut from its immemorial stage, will all but touch a brand new building which soars indifferently skywards. No less of a monument to our present way of life, it houses the *Financial Times*.

Postscript

No advocate for the insertion of texts into their material context, or proponent of the case for a 'conversation' that accompanies and finally constitutes the construction of cultural meaning, could have wished for a more apposite conclusion than the one supplied by the correspondence which followed the initial publication of the above piece. The combative process of 'meaning by' has had few better manifestations than that offered by the writers of the letters to the editor of the *London Review of Books* detailed below. It is entirely apt that they should finally elbow me off the page:

> 22 March 1990 (James Wood); 19 April 1990 (Alan Sinfield); 24 May 1990 (James Wood); 14 June 1990 (John Drakakis, Alan Sinfield); 28 June 1990 (Graham Martin); 12 July 1990 (Boris Ford); 26 July 1990 (Alan Sinfield); 16 August 1990 (James Wood); 30 August 1990 (M. J. Devaney, Michael Taylor); 13 September 1990 (Malcolm Evans); 20 December 1990 (John Caird); 7 February 1991 (Anthony Pratt); 7 March 1991 (Alan Sinfield); 4 April 1991 (Bernard Bergonzi); 25 April 1991 (James Wood); 23 May 1991 (Penny McCarthy, Alan Sinfield); 13 June 1991 (Martin Orkin, Leonard Jackson); 11 July 1991 (Alan Sinfield, Michael Rosen); 15 August 1991 (Ania Loomba); 12 September 1991 (James Wood).

Notes

1 By

1 See *Hamlet*, ed. Harold Jenkins (Arden edn), London, Routledge, 1982, p. 296. See also pp. 505–6 where the meanings of *miching malicho* are fully discussed.

2 See my 'The institutionalization of literature: the university', in Martin Coyle, Peter Garside, Malcolm Kelsall and John Peck (eds), *Encyclopedia of Literature and Criticism*, London, Routledge, 1990, pp. 926–38.

3 See Richard Rorty, *Philosophy and the Mirror of Nature*, Oxford, Blackwell, 1980, p. 9 and pp. 357–94, where a crucial distinction between 'systematic' and 'edifying' philosophy is proposed. Further, related considerations are dealt with in Rorty's essays 'Philosophy as a kind of writing', and 'Pragmatism, relativism and irrationalism', in *Consequences of Pragmatism*, Brighton, Harvester Press, 1982, pp. 90–109 and 160–75, and the first two chapters of *Contingency, Irony and Solidarity*, Cambridge, Cambridge University Press, 1989. The essays 'Solidarity or objectivity?' and 'Texts and lumps' in *Objectivity, Relativism and Truth: Philosophical Papers*, vol. 1, Cambridge, Cambridge University Press, 1991, pp. 21–34 and 78–92 are also relevant.

4 See Rorty, 1980, op. cit., p. 378. The essay 'The priority of democracy to philosophy' (in Rorty, 1991, op. cit., pp. 175–96) relates the abandonment of the 'spectator theory of knowledge' to the needs of a democratic society. See also his 'Just one more species doing its best' in *The London Review of Books* 13(14) (25 July 1991), pp. 3–7.

5 The work of Stanley Fish is also important here, particularly aspects of his notion of 'interpretive [*sic*] communities' proposed in *Is There a Text in This Class?*, Cambridge, Mass., Harvard University Press, 1980, and elsewhere. In practice 'interpretive communities' consist of groupings within societies formed by the discursively like-minded. In such communities, the act of interpretation will 'constitute, more or less in agreement, the same text, although the sameness would not be attributable to the self-identity of the text, but to the communal nature of the interpretive act' (*Doing What Comes Naturally*, Oxford, Oxford University Press, 1989, p. 141). For Fish, a Rorty-esque 'conversation' can take place in so far as the communities are not static and the consciousness of their members is not irrecoverably frozen into a specific shape.

Far from it, Fish argues. The communities constitute the very 'engines of change whose work is at the same time assimilative and self-transforming' (ibid., p. 152). Of course, this gives a rather special sense to the notion of 'change', limiting it to manoeuvres presupposed by the communities' existing structures. See Rorty's discussion of Fish in the essay 'Texts and lumps', op. cit. Cf. my comments on Fish and on Umberto Eco's *The Limits of Interpretation*, Bloomington, Indiana, Indiana University Press, 1990, in 'Is there anything there out there?', *Times Literary Supplement*, 1 February 1991, p. 9.

2   Or

1 See T. Walter Herbert, *Oberon's Mazed World*, Baton Rouge, Louisiana State University Press, 1977, p. 16.
2 See Louis Montrose, '"Shaping fantasies": figurations of gender and power in Elizabethan culture', in Stephen Greenblatt (ed.), *Representing the English Renaissance*, Berkeley, University of California Press, 1988, pp. 31–64. See especially p. 40.
3 Richard Levin, 'The poetics and politics of Bardicide', *PMLA*, 105(3) (1990), pp. 491–504.
4 Coppélia Kahn, 'The absent mother in *King Lear*', in Margaret Ferguson, Maureen Quilligan and Nancy Vickers (eds), *Rewriting the Renaissance: The Discourses of Sexual Difference in Early Modern Europe*, Chicago, University of Chicago Press, 1986, pp. 33–49.
5 See Montrose, op. cit., p. 32. Also *A Midsummer Night's Dream*, ed. Harold F. Brooks (Arden edn), London, Routledge, 1979, pp. liii, lv.
6 See Mary Beth Rose, 'Where are the mothers in Shakespeare? Options for gender representation in the English Renaissance', *Shakespeare Quarterly* 42(3) (Fall 1991), pp. 291–314.
7 Cf. Montrose, op. cit., p. 53.
8 See Glynne Wickham, 'From tragedy to tragi-comedy, *King Lear* as prologue', *Shakespeare Survey* 26 (1973), pp. 33–48. See also p. 124–5 in this volume.
9 Montrose, op. cit., p. 46. Cf. Coppélia Kahn's judgement concerning *King Lear*, a play in which 'The only source of love, power and authority is the father – an awesome, demanding presence', op. cit., p. 36. Mary Beth Rose's extremely fruitful essay seems to miss Nedar's potential altogether, announcing that 'in the six most celebrated romantic comedies (*Love's Labour's Lost, The Taming of the Shrew, A Midsummer Night's Dream, As You Like It, Much Ado About Nothing*, and *Twelfth Night*) no mothers appear at all', although she does register that a 'ghost' mother, Innogen, appears in the stage directions in the early printed texts of *Much Ado* (ibid., p. 292). However, her conclusion that, in Elizabethan terms, mothers tend to be marginalized or erased, that the desirable adult society is deliberately 'construed as motherless', and that the 'best mother is an absent or dead mother' is very much to the point here. The article as a whole is a mine of valuable information. See especially pp. 301–2, 307, 312. Nedar's role as a mother who is at once 'erased' and 'asserted' (see p. 312) certainly enacts a contemporary paradox to which Professor Rose rightly draws attention, and on that basis I might perhaps

query her statement that 'Shakespeare's drama fails either to reproduce or to appropriate these representations' (ibid., p. 313).

10 See David Young, *Something of Great Constancy: the Art of A Midsummer Night's Dream*, New Haven, Yale University Press, 1966, pp. 70–1.

11 Cited in John Dover Wilson (ed.), *A Midsummer Night's Dream*, Cambridge, Cambridge University Press, 1924, pp. 141–2.

12 See ibid., p. 142.

13 David Young, op. cit., p. 71.

14 Dover Wilson, op. cit., pp. 80–6.

15 Germaine Greer's *The Change: Women, Ageing and the Menopause*, London, Hamish Hamilton, 1991, gives a full and combative account of the situation. See especially pp. 213–44.

16 See Eric A. Havelock, *Preface to Plato*, New York, Grosset & Dunlap, 1967 (first pub. Cambridge, Mass., Harvard University Press, 1963), p. x.

17 Matie Molinaro, Corinne McLuhan and William Toye (eds), *Letters of Marshall McLuhan*, Oxford, Oxford University Press, 1987, pp. 416–19.

18 McLuhan, ibid., pp. 510, 525.

19 A 'forme' is a term associated with printing, and refers to a body of type secured in a chase and ready for use.

20 I am drawing heavily here on Edward W. Said's authoritative discussion of the complexities which characterize relationships of filiation and affiliation. See his *The World, The Text, and The Critic*, London, Faber & Faber, 1984, pp. 16–25, 174–7, and *passim*. The essay 'On repetition' (ibid., pp. 11–25) is particularly relevant.

21 Ovid, *Metamorphoses*, 1, 1–176, XV, 879. I am using the translation by Mary M. Innes, Harmondsworth, Penguin, 1955. See pp. 29–33 and 357.

22 Harry Levin, 'Shakespeare's nomenclature', in Gerald W. Chapman (ed.), *Essays on Shakespeare*, Princeton, Princeton University Press, 1965, pp. 59–90. See p. 76. Cf. William C. Carroll, *The Metamorphoses of Shakespearean Comedy*, Princeton, Princeton University Press, 1985, pp. 32ff.

23 Cited in T. Walter Herbert, op. cit., p. 31.

24 Bertolt Brecht, 'On experimental theatre', in *Brecht on Theatre*, trans. and ed. John Willett, London, Methuen, 1964, p. 132.

25 *Metamorphoses*, IV, 28–63, op.cit., p. 95.

26 Montrose, op. cit., pp. 51–2, 63n.

27 Steven Mullaney, *The Place of the Stage: License Play and Power in Renaissance England*, Chicago and London, University of Chicago Press, 1988, *passim*.

28 ibid., pp. 8, 20–1.

29 ibid., p. 51.

30 ibid., p. 40.

31 Cf. Annabel Patterson's provocative reading of *A Midsummer Night's Dream* against the background of contemporary riots: *Shakespeare and the Popular Voice*, Oxford, Blackwell, 1989, pp. 52–70. Also, see below, pp. 143–6.

32 See Michel Foucault, 'The order of discourse', in Robert Young (ed.), *Untying the Text*, London, Routledge, 1981, pp. 48–78. See especially pp. 56–7.

33 Said, op. cit., p. 20.

34   ibid., p. 16.
35   Foucault, op. cit., p. 58.
36   See Jonathan Bate's excellent account of Hazlitt's criticism, from which
     these and the following quotations derive, *Shakespearean Constitutions:
     Politics, Theatre, Criticism 1730–1830*, Oxford, Clarendon Press, 1989, p.
     165. See below, pp. 44, 143.
37   Cited in Bate, ibid., p. 166.
38   ibid., p. 177.
39   See George Dangerfield, *The Strange Death of Liberal England, 1919–1914*,
     New York, Capricorn Books, 1961 (first pub. 1935), p. 395.
40   ibid., p. 368.
41   Emmeline Pankhurst, *My Own Story*, London, Eveleigh Nash, 1914, pp.
     335–6.
42   ibid., p. 554.
43   Dangerfield, op. cit., p. 377.
44   ibid.
45   Lillah McCarthy (Lady Keeble), *Myself and My Friends*, London, Thornton
     Butterworth, 1933, p. 174.
46   E. Sylvia Pankhurst, *The Suffragette Movement*, London, Longmans & Co.,
     1931, p. 284.
47   Emmeline Pankhurst, op.cit., p. 114.
48   McCarthy, op. cit., pp. 148–9.
49   ibid., p. 149.
50   ibid., p. 161.
51   See Oscar Wilde, 'The critic as artist', in *The Artist as Critic: Critical
     Writings of Oscar Wilde*, ed. Richard Ellmann, London, W. H. Allen, 1970,
     pp. 340–408.
52   See Terence Hawkes, *That Shakespeherian Rag*, London, Methuen, 1986,
     pp 122–4.
53   See David McLellan, *The Thought of Karl Marx*, London, Macmillan, 1971,
     pp. 60–4.
54   Said, op. cit., p. 124. Said's whole account of *The Eighteenth Brumaire* (pp.
     121–5) is extremely valuable and I have made extensive use of it here.
     The distinction drawn between this and Kierkegaard's *Repetition* is also
     helpful and provocative: see pp. 120–1.
55   See E. K. Chambers, *William Shakespeare, A Study of Facts and Problems*,
     vol. II, Oxford, Oxford University Press, 1930, p. 298; and S. Schoenbaum,
     Shakespeare's Lives, Oxford, Oxford University Press, 1970, pp. 159, 190.

3   Shakespeare and the General Strike

1   Fredric Jameson, *The Political Unconscious: Narrative as a Socially Symbolic
    Act*, London, Routledge, 1981, p. 193.
2   See *Coriolanus*, ed. Philip Brockbank (Arden edn), London, Routledge,
    1976, p. 26.
3   See Jonathan Bate, *Shakespearean Constitutions: Politics, Theatre, Criticism
    1730–1830*, Oxford, Clarendon Press, 1989, pp. 160–78.
4   Charlotte Brontë, *Shirley*, London, Dent, Everyman's Library, 1955 (first
    pub. 1849), pp. 70–2.

5 See Oscar James Campbell and Edward G. Quinn (eds), *The Reader's Encyclopedia of Shakespeare*, New York, Crowell, 1966, pp. 146–7. Also *Coriolanus*, op. cit., pp. 84–6.

6 See Bertolt Brecht, 'A study of the first scene of Shakespeare's *Coriolanus*', in *Brecht on Theatre*, trans. and ed. John Willett, London, Methuen, 1964, pp. 252–65.

7 See Günter Grass, *The Plebeians Rehearse the Uprising: A German Tragedy*, trans. Ralph Mannheim (with an introductory address by the author), London, Secker & Warburg, 1967.

8 Christopher Farman, *The General Strike*, 2nd edn, London, Panther Books, 1974 (first pub. 1972), p. 42.

9 See Richard Griffiths, *Fellow Travellers of the Right*, London, Constable, 1980, pp. 85–6.

10 ibid., p. 86.

11 ibid.

12 Farman, op. cit., p. 46.

13 ibid., pp. 54–6.

14 ibid., p. 81.

15 ibid., p. 72.

16 See Griffiths, op. cit., pp. 354–5.

17 ibid., p. 24. See also *The London Mercury*, May 1926, pp. 1–2.

18 *The Times*, 23 April 1926, p. 12.

19 *The Times*, 24 April 1926, p. 10.

20 See Thomas Jones, *Whitehall Diary*, vol. II, ed. Keith Middlemass, Oxford, Oxford University Press, 1969, pp. 18–19.

21 See J. P. Stern, *Hitler: the Führer and the People*, London, Fontana, 1975, pp. 43–4.

22 See *Coriolanus*, op. cit., pp. 8, 308.

23 ibid., p. 82.

4 Take me to your Leda

1 A. J. P. Taylor, *English History 1914–1945*, Oxford, Oxford University Press, 1965, p. 268. For MacDonald's words see p. 285.

2 For an account of Wilson Knight's 'Modernism', see Hugh Grady's ground-breaking *The Modernist Shakespeare*, Oxford, Oxford University Press, 1991, pp. 74–112. See also my comments in chapter 5, pp. 95–6.

3 G. Wilson Knight, *The Wheel of Fire*, revised edn, London, Methuen, 1954 (first pub. London, Oxford University Press, 1930; revised edn first pub. 1949), pp. 76, 80–1, 87, 90–1.

4 William Empson, *Seven Types of Ambiguity*, 3rd edn, Harmondsworth, Penguin, 1961 (first pub. London, Chatto & Windus, 1930; 2nd edn 1947), p. 184.

5 ibid., p. 184.

6 *Scrutiny* 10(3) (Winter 1942), pp. 222–33.

7 Cf. Rebecca West, *The Meaning of Treason*, London, Macmillan, 1949, pp. 235 and 238 on the case of the wartime traitor Stoker Rose, whom she casts as Claudio in *Measure for Measure*.

8 F. R. Leavis, 'The greatness of *Measure for Measure*', *Scrutiny* 10(3) (Winter 1942), pp. 234–47.

9 ibid., p. 243.
10 ibid., p. 236.
11 ibid., p. 234.
12 ibid., p. 241.
13 ibid., p. 246.
14 Cited in Francis Mulhern, *The Moment of Scrutiny*, London, New Left Books, 1979, pp. 3–4.
15 F. R. Leavis, 'Memories of Wittgenstein', *The Human World* 10 (February 1973), pp. 66–79. (The essay is reprinted in F. R. Leavis, *The Critic as Anti-Philosopher*, ed. G. Singh, London, Chatto & Windus, 1982, pp. 129–45.)
16 ibid., pp. 78–9.
17 See Ernest Schanzer, 'The marriage-contracts in *Measure for Measure*', *Shakespeare Survey* 13 (1960), pp. 81–9.
18 Ludwig Wittgenstein, *Culture and Value (Vermischte Bemerkungen)*, ed. G. H. Von Wright and Heikki Nyman, trans. Peter Winch, Oxford, Blackwell, 1980, p. 49e. My attention was first drawn to this material by George Steiner. See his *Reading Against Shakespeare* (The W. P. Ker Lecture, 1986), Glasgow, The University Press, 1987.
19 Wittgenstein, op. cit., p. 49e.
20 ibid., p. 84e.
21 ibid., p. 85e.
22 *Scrutiny* 10(4) (Spring 1942), p. 328.
23 *Scrutiny* 13(3) (Autumn–Winter 1945), p. 234. See also *Scrutiny* 12(3) (Summer 1944), pp. 222–7; and *Scrutiny* 13(1) (Spring 1945), pp. 72–3.
24 Leavis, op. cit., p. 72.
25 Richard Rorty, 'The contingency of language', *London Review of Books* 8(7) (17 April 1986), pp. 3–6.

5 Slow, slow, quick quick, slow

1 See A. J. Eagleston, 'Wordsworth, Coleridge and the spy', in E. Blunden and E. L. Griggs (eds), *Coleridge: Studies by Several Hands*, London, Constable, 1934, pp. 71–87.
2 See Kathleen Coburn (ed.), *The Collected Works of Samuel Taylor Coleridge*, vol. 7, *Biographia Literaria 1*, Princeton, Princeton University Press, 1983, pp. 193–5.
3 ibid.
4 See Robin Winks, *Cloak and Gown: Scholars in America's Secret War*, London, Collins Harvill, 1987, pp. 11–59 and *passim*. Also William H. Epstein, 'Counter intelligence: Cold War criticism and eighteenth century studies', *English Literary History* 57 (1990), pp. 63–99.
5 Julian Maclaren-Ross, *Memoirs of the Forties*, Harmondsworth, Penguin, 1984, pp. 22–3.
6 Cited in William Allison and John Fairley, *The Monocled Mutineer*, London, Quartet, 1978, paperback edn. 1979, pp. 67–8.
7 ibid., p. 57. See the whole account, pp. 44ff.
8 ibid., pp. 56–7.
9 Cf. Michel Foucault's classic discussion of these and other relevant issues in *Discipline and Punish: The Birth of the Prison*, trans. Alan Sheridan,

Harmondsworth, Penguin, 1979. The chapters 'The body of the condemned' and 'The spectacle of the scaffold' (pp. 3–69) are particularly relevant.

10 Jean Cocteau, *Journal*, 8 June 1952. Cited in *The Independent*, London (15 June 1991), p. 30. Cf. *Past Tense: Diaries/Jean Cocteau*, trans. Richard Howard: vol. 1, London, Hamish Hamilton, 1987; vol. 2, London, Methuen, 1990.

11 See the *Dictionary of National Biography 1971–80*, Oxford, Oxford University Press, 1986. Also Ian Whitcomb, *After the Ball*, Harmondsworth, Penguin, 1973 (first pub. London, Allen Lane, 1972) pp. 177–8. As I write, I am delighted to discover that my research student from Singapore, Victor Neo, was named after Silvester.

12 See *Dictionary of National Biography*, op. cit. Also, Victor Silvester, *Dancing is My Life*, London, Heinemann, 1958. Silvester's peculiar involvement in the trial for treason of a British officer, Norman Baillie-Stewart, is perhaps also worth pondering. See Rebecca West, *The Meaning of Treason*, London, Macmillan, 1949, pp. 207–8.

13 See my *That Shakespeherian Rag*, London, Methuen, 1986, p. 121. Also my 'The institutionalization of literature: the university', in Martin Coyle, Peter Garside, Malcolm Kelsall and John Peck (eds), *Encyclopedia of Literature and Criticism*, London, Routledge, 1990, pp. 926–38.

14 Valerie Eliot (ed.), *The Letters of T. S. Eliot*, vol. 1, London, Faber & Faber, 1988, p. xxi. (Hereafter referred to as *Letters*.)

15 *Letters*, p. 39.

16 *Letters*, p. 70.

17 *Letters*, p. 97.

18 ibid.

19 Dated by Grover Smith, *T. S. Eliot's Poetry and Plays: A Study in Sources and Meaning*, 2nd edn, Chicago, University of Chicago Press, 1974 (first pub. 1956), p. 31.

20 *Letters*, p. 97.

21 ibid.

22 T. S. Matthews, *Great Tom: Notes Towards the Definition of T. S. Eliot*, London, Weidenfeld & Nicolson, 1974, p. 53. Vivien's name was spelt differently from time to time, even by those who knew her.

23 *Letters*, p. 275.

24 Lyndall Gordon, *Eliot's Early Years*, Oxford, Oxford University Press, 1977, p. 75. See also Bernard Bergonzi, *T. S. Eliot*, London, Macmillan, 1972, p. 85.

25 See 'Feiron Morris', 'Thé Dansant', *The Criterion* 3(9) (October 1924), p. 74. I am forbidden by the Eliot Estate to quote from this story. However, it is available to readers, apparently without restriction, as indicated.

26 Matthews, op. cit., p. 53.

27 *Letters*, p. 58.

28 *Letters*, p. 460.

29 E. M. Forster, *Abinger Harvest*, London, Edward Arnold, 1953 (first pub. 1936), p. 112.

30 T. S. Eliot, *Selected Essays*, 3rd edn, London, Faber & Faber, 1951, pp. 141–6.

31 T. S. Eliot, *The Use of Poetry and the Use of Criticism*, London, Faber & Faber, 1964 (first pub. 1933), p. 44.

32 G. Wilson Knight, *The Wheel of Fire*, revised edn, London, Methuen, 1954 (first pub. London, Oxford University Press, 1930; revised edn first pub. 1949), p. 3.

33 See Hugh Grady, *The Modernist Shakespeare*, Oxford, Oxford University Press, 1991, pp. 93–4.

34 ibid., p. 105.

35 ibid., p. 111.

36 Cited in Frank Kermode, *The Romantic Image*, London, Routledge, 1957, pp. 72–3.

37 ibid., p. 52. See pp. 49–91 for a full discussion of this issue.

38 W. B. Yeats, *Autobiographies*, London, Macmillan, 1955, p. 292. See the discussion of the paintings in Edward Engelberg, *The Vast Design: Patterns in W. B. Yeats's Aesthetic*, Toronto, University of Toronto Press, 1964, pp. 85–6. I am drawing here on the central points powerfully made by Frank Kermode, op. cit., pp. 49–91.

39 See *Coriolanus*, ed. Philip Brockbank (Arden edn), London, Routledge, 1976, pp. 346–8.

40 Alexander Barclay, (trans.) *The Ship of Fools* (1509), ed. T.H. Jamieson, Edinburgh, William Paterson, London, Henry Sotheran, 1874, vol. I, pp. 293–5.

41 I am drawing here on John Drakakis, 'The plays of Shackerley Marmion', unpublished Ph.D. dissertation, University of Leeds, 1989, pp. 507ff., esp. 527, 533, 549.

42 *Lucian*, trans. A. M. Harmon, London, Heinemann (*The Loeb Classical Library*, 1913, p. 219.

43 Sir Thomas Elyot, *The Boke Named the Governour*, London, Dent, Everyman's Library, 1907 (first pub. 1531), p. 86.

44 ibid., pp. 86, 94–5.

45 Drakakis, op. cit., p. 537.

46 See Robert Krueger (ed.), *The Poems of Sir John Davies*, Oxford, Oxford University Press, 1975, p. 94.

47 See Philip Brockbank's comments, *Coriolanus*, op. cit., p. 38.

48 ibid., p. 318.

49 ibid., p. 328.

50 I am forbidden by the Eliot Estate to quote from this poem. However, it is printed in full and discussed in detail in H. A. Mason's 'Eliot's *Ode*: a neglected poem?', *The Cambridge Quarterly* 19(4) (1990), pp. 304–35. Grover Smith calls it 'Eliot's nadir', Grover Smith, op. cit., p. 38.

51 See Hawkes, op. cit., pp. 60ff.

52 *Letters*, p. 159.

53 *Letters*, pp. 173–4.

54 *The New Statesman*, 12 May 1917, p. 140. See *Letters*, p. 179.

55 *The Times*, 4 July 1918, p. 5.

56 *Letters*, p. 363.

57 *Letters*, pp. 264–5.

58 See Grover Smith, op. cit., p. 162.

59 *Letters*, pp. 264–5.

60 *Letters*, p. 337.

61 This point is well made by Leah S. Marcus, *Puzzling Shakespeare: Local Reading and its Discontents*, Berkeley, University of California Press, 1988, p. 206.

62 Cited in Charles Seymour, 'Woodrow Wilson', *Dictionary of American Biography*, vol. XX, London, Humphrey Milford/Oxford University Press, 1936, p. 364.
63 *Letters*, p. 310.
64 *Letters*, pp. 392, 402.
65 *Letters*, p. 431.
66 For alternative readings see Grover Smith, op. cit., pp. 37–8.
67 See *Letters*, pp. 511–15.
68 *Times Literary Supplement*, 21 September 1940, p. 483.
69 Eliot, *Selected Essays*, 1951, op. cit., p. 287.
70 F. R. Leavis, 'T. S. Eliot and the life of English Literature', in *Valuation in Criticism and Other Essays*, ed. G. Singh, Cambridge, Cambridge University Press, 1986; see especially pp. 131–3.
71 Cf. Lyndall Gordon on the connection Eliot makes between burning and dancing in *Eliot's New Life*, Oxford, Oxford University Press, 1988, p. 101. See also Bergonzi, op. cit., pp. 168–9.
72 See Paul de Man, *Blindness and Insight: Essays in the Rhetoric of Contemporary Criticism*, 2nd revised edn, Minneapolis, University of Minnesota Press, 1983, pp. 147–8. De Man's personal reasons for wishing 'to wipe out whatever came earlier' were of course served by such views, and it is significant that America gave him the opportunity to do so. See also the extremely interesting discussion in Marshall Berman's *All That Is Solid Melts Into Air*, London, Verso, 1983, *passim*, esp. p. 331.
73 Peter Ackroyd, *T. S. Eliot*, London, Hamish Hamilton, 1984, p. 89.

6 Lear's maps

1 Leonard Tennenhouse, *Power on Display: the Politics of Shakespeare's Genres*, London and New York, Routledge, 1986, p. 10. The whole range of Tennenhouse's argument deserves study and what follows is greatly indebted to it. Cf. my 'Uses and abuses of the Bard', *Times Literary Supplement*, 10 April 1987, pp. 390–3.
2 I am here drawing extensively on Glynne Wickham, 'From tragedy to tragi-comedy, *King Lear* as prologue', *Shakespeare Survey* 26 (1973), pp. 33–48.
3 See Hugh Grady, *The Modernist Shakespeare*, Oxford, Oxford University Press, 1991, pp. 225–35. The whole section is relevant to what follows, and I have drawn on it extensively.
4 See Grady, ibid., p. 229.
5 The tendency to offer a positivist, totalizing view of history in which authority and containment are triumphant has been carefully discussed by Stephen Greenblatt in *Shakespearean Negotiations: the Circulation of Social Energy in Renaissance England*, Oxford, Oxford University Press, 1988. See pp. 2–20. See also Grady, op. cit., pp. 229–30.
6 See Terry Eagleton (ed.), *Raymond Williams: Critical Perspectives*, Oxford, Polity Press, 1989, pp. 165–75.
7 See Jonathan Dollimore and Alan Sinfield (eds), *Political Shakespeare: New Essays in Cultural Materialism*, Manchester, Manchester University Press, 1985, p. viii.

8 Raymond Williams, *Marxism and Literature*, Oxford, Oxford University Press, 1977, pp. 121–7.

9 Jonathan Dollimore, in Stanley Wells (ed.), *Shakespeare: a Bibliographical Guide*, Oxford, Oxford University Press, 1990, p. 414.

10 Jonathan Dollimore, 'Shakespeare, Cultural Materialism, Feminism and Marxist Humanism', *New Literary History* 21 (1989–90), p. 472.

11 See Grady's comments on this point: Grady, op. cit., pp. 234–5.

12 Dollimore, 1989–90, op. cit., p. 482.

13 Frank Lentricchia, *Criticism and Social Change*, Chicago, University of Chicago Press, 1983, p. 15.

14 Dollimore and Sinfield (eds), op. cit., p. viii.

15 ibid.

16 I am drawing on Hallam Fordham's account of the production, as recorded in his *Player in Action: John Gielgud as 'King Lear' (with notes by John Gielgud). A record of John Gielgud's performance as 'King Lear' at the Old Vic Theatre, London 1940*, Typescript, Catalogue no. Tb 17, Folger Shakespeare Library, Washington DC, 1940, pp. 1, i (1–4). Fordham states that 'Throughout the run of the play, and at certain stages of its preparation, I was able to study and record the production in general and Gielgud's performance in particular, on many occasions' (Foreword). See also Christine Dymkowski's detailed discussion of this production in her valuable *Harley Granville Barker: a Preface to Modern Shakespeare*, London and Toronto, Associated University Presses, 1986, pp. 148–50.

17 'Let the audience see plainly at once who each character is. H. G. B.' This is inscribed in red at the bottom of this page: i.e. p. 1, i (2).

18 John Gielgud, *An Actor and His Time*, London, Sidgwick & Jackson, 1979, p. 136. Further information is to be found in John Gielgud, *Stage Directions*, London, Heinemann, 1963, pp. 51–5, 121–33.

19 See *The Listener*, 30 May 1940, p. 1036.

20 Paul Rabinow (ed.), *The Foucault Reader*, Harmondsworth, Penguin, 1984, p. 22.

21 Lewis Casson, preface to C. B. Purdom, *Harley Granville Barker: Man of the Theatre, Dramatist and Scholar*, London, Rockliff, 1955, p. viii.

22 In respect of the moment I have been focusing on, the distinction between the Quarto and Folio versions is not insignificant:

Q1 (1608):

Lear: Meane time we will expresse our darker purposes,
         The map there; know we have divided
         In three, our kingdome; and tis our first intent,
         To shake all cares and busines of our state,
         Confirming them on yonger years

FI (1623):

Lear: Meane time we shall express our darker purpose.
         Give me the map there [F3, F4, 'here']. Know that we have divided
         In three our kingdom: and 'tis our fast intent
         To shake all cares and business from our age
         Conferring them on younger strengths

23 See Grady's excellent analysis of this point: Grady, op. cit., pp. 229–30. See also Howard Felperin, *The Uses of the Canon: Elizabethan Literature and Contemporary Theory*, Oxford, Oxford University Press, 1990, for a perceptive interrogation of this issue.
24 See Lentricchia's discussion of this point, op. cit., pp. 131ff.

7 Bardbiz

1 This piece appeared in slightly different form in *The London Review of Books*, 22 February 1990. It focused on the following volumes:
Andrew Gurr with John Orrell, *Rebuilding Shakespeare's Globe*, London, Weidenfeld & Nicolson, 1989.
Annabel Patterson, *Shakespeare and the Popular Voice*, Oxford, Blackwell, 1989.
Gary Taylor, *Reinventing Shakespeare*, London, The Hogarth Press, 1990.
Michael D. Bristol, *Shakespeare's America. America's Shakespeare*, London, Routledge, 1990.
Reference was also made to the following works:
Jonathan Bate, *Shakespearean Constitutions: Politics, Theatre, Criticism 1730–1830*, Oxford, Clarendon Press, 1989.
Malcolm Evans, *Signifying Nothing: Truth's True Contents in Shakespeare's Texts*, 2nd edn, Brighton, Harvester Wheatsheaf, 1990.
Jonathan Dollimore, *Radical Tragedy: Religion, Ideology and Power in the Drama of Shakespeare and his Contemporaries*, 2nd edn, Brighton, Harvester Wheatsheaf, 1990.
2 Thomas Hobbes, *Leviathan*, 1651, part II, chapter 29.

Index